D1434066

DEPRESSIVE DISORDERS IN DIFFERENT CULTURES

Report on the WHO Collaborative Study on Standardized Assessment of Depressive Disorders

N. Sartorius,   H. Davidian,   G. Ernberg,   F. R. Fenton,
I. Fujii,   M. Gastpar,   W. Gulbinat,   A. Jablensky,
P. Kielholz,   H. E. Lehmann,   M. Naraghi,   M. Shimizu,
N. Shinfuku,   R. Takahashi

WORLD HEALTH ORGANIZATION
GENEVA
1983

ISBN 92 4 156075 4

PRINTED IN ENGLAND

81/5158 – Spottiswoode Ballantyne – 6500

CONTENTS

Collaborators and acknowledgements

This report is based on data and experience obtained in the framework of the WHO Collaborative Study on the Assessment of Depressive Disorders, a project sponsored and funded by the World Health Organization and the participating field research centres. The collaborating institutions and investigators in this study have been:

Basle (Switzerland)
University Psychiatric Clinic, Basle; and Cantonal Psychiatric Hospital, Weissenau.
Dr P. Kielholz (*Chief Investigator*), Dr M. Gastpar, Dr G. Hole

Montreal (Canada)
Department of Psychiatry, McGill University; Douglas Hospital Centre; and Montreal General Hospital.
Dr H. E. Lehmann (*Chief Investigator*), Dr F. R. Fenton, Dr R. Lajoie, Dr S. Ang, Dr R. Yassa

Nagasaki (Japan)
Department of Neuropsychiatry, Nagasaki University School of Medicine.
Dr R. Takahashi (*Chief Investigator*), Dr I. Fujii, Dr Y. Sakurai, Dr T. Yuzuriha

Teheran (Iran)
Department of Psychiatry, Roozbeh Hospital.
Dr H. Davidian (*Chief Investigator*), Dr M. Naraghi

Tokyo (Japan)
Department of Psychiatry, Jikei University Hospital.
Dr N. Shinfuku (*Chief Investigator*), Dr K. Hasegawa, Dr M. Shimizu

Geneva (Switzerland)
Division of Mental Health, World Health Organization.
Dr N. Sartorius (*Principal Investigator*), Dr A. Jablensky (*Chief Headquarters Investigator*), Mr W. Gulbinat, Mrs G. Ernberg

*   *   *

The technical assistance of Mr Trung Ngo Khac, the secretarial assistance of Mrs S. Fischer, Mrs V. Cimato, and Miss G. Sykes, and the editorial help of Dr J. Gallagher, are gratefully acknowledged.

Introduction

Each year at least 100 million people in the world develop clinically recognizable depression and for several reasons the number is likely to increase (Sartorius, 1979). For one reason, life expectancy is increasing in most countries and both the absolute numbers and the proportions of people at risk of developing depression are accordingly also increasing. For another, more people are now living in a rapidly changing social and physical environment that often gives rise to acute or prolonged psychosocial stress and may lead to depressive reactions. At a time when traditional protective mechanisms of social groups are breaking down and many people are exposed to the unsettling effects of uprooting, family disintegration, and social isolation, the prevalence of depressive disorders arising as a response to stressful psychosocial factors (Brown & Harris, 1978) is likely to increase. A third reason is that there is now an increase in morbidity from chronic cardiovascular diseases, collagen diseases, gastroenteric diseases, and cerebrovascular and other neurological disorders, and these have been shown to be associated with depressive reactions in as many as 20% of all cases (Sartorius, 1976). If the prevalence of these organic disorders continues its upward trend (which is likely, with the increase in longeval populations) an increase in the frequency of somatogenic depressive disorders must also be expected. Whether this increase will be offset by fewer cases of somatogenic depression associated with acute physical illnesses—such as infectious diseases—cannot be determined at present. A fourth major reason for the predicted increase in depressive disorders is the greatly increased use of a variety of medicaments and alcohol (Mullinger et al., 1978; Craig & van Natta, 1978). Certain drugs whose consumption is now steadily growing are known to precipitate or exacerbate depression; among them are sedatives and tranquilizers, antihypertensive drugs, and various hormone preparations.

There are thus several reasons to justify the prediction of a genuine increase in the prevalence of depressive disorders. However, true prevalence often affects planning in health less than impressions ("apparent prevalence") do; in the case of depression there are good grounds for believing that the apparent prevalence will also show an increase. More patients suffering from depression are at present likely to seek treatment, and the invisible part of the

1

"iceberg" of depressive illness in the community which, according to Shepherd (1979), comprises up to 98% of all cases, may thus be reduced. Physicians are showing a greater readiness to diagnose depression, probably because treatment is now more likely to be successful. New diagnostic concepts, such as that of masked depression, are gaining wider acceptance and their use is adding to the statistics of depression cases that would not have been so classified previously (Kielholz, 1979). In many of the developing countries that are becoming increasingly urbanized, more patients—when faced with the problems of describing their symptoms to a physician—are becoming able to express in words their experience of depression more accurately, as German (1972), for example, has shown in his studies.

An illustration of what is probably the combined effect of all these trends is provided by an inquiry among general practitioners in several European countries (Pöldinger, 1974). Between 73 and 90% of respondents in Austria, West Berlin, the Federal Republic of Germany, France, and Switzerland had the impression that the prevalence of depression in their everyday practice was increasing, and most of them reported that at least 10% of all the patients they saw in a year had depressive illnesses.

Although the size of the problem is now better recognized and effective treatment is available, most of the world's depressive patients remain untreated and thus exposed to unnecessary suffering and disablement; their families and communities also suffer major losses. This situation is particularly severe in the developing countries, although the number of untreated but treatable cases is far from trivial in the industrialized countries too. There are many reasons for this, ranging from poorly trained health workers and scarce resources, hindering the provision of effective medicaments; to insufficient knowledge about the nature, frequency, and management of depressive disorders.

The Mental Health Programme of the World Health Organization has as one of its main objectives the prevention and treatment of psychiatric and neurological disorders. To achieve it a two-pronged strategy has been adopted: firstly, major attention has been given to promoting the application in national health programmes of available knowledge through the development of decentralized mental health services integrated with general health services; and secondly, multidisciplinary research is being stimulated and coordinated, with the aim of bringing together scientists from different parts of the world and accelerating the process of acquisition of new knowledge.

The first step in effecting this strategy as it concerns depressive disorders was the development and promotion of a common language to facilitate communication among mental health workers in the field. Since the mid-1960s WHO has initiated several projects to develop internationally acceptable methods for the assessment, classification, and reporting of depressive disorders. The WHO programme on the standardization of psychiatric diagnosis and classification, in which groups of experts from many countries are collaborating, produced the proposals for the mental disorders section of the Ninth Revision of the International Classification of Diseases (WHO, 1978), which unlike earlier revisions contains a larger number of rubrics for the classification of depressive conditions and a companion glossary. In another project concerned with the prevention of suicide, efforts were made to discover the reasons for unreliability in the reporting of suicide and attempted suicide (WHO, 1974).

In another major collaborative study (the International Pilot Study of Schizophrenia, WHO, 1973; 1979), over 1200 patients in nine countries were assessed with standardized methods and followed up over five years. Although its main focus was on schizophrenic disorders, a total of 256 patients with depressive conditions were included as a comparison group. The results indicated, firstly, that standardized techniques can be developed for assessing patients with severe mental disorders—including depression—in different cultures; and secondly, that psychiatrists educated in different traditions and schools can be trained to apply such techniques uniformly and reliably. The use of standardized techniques demonstrated that depressive patients identified in nine very different cultures had many characteristics in common, and formed a group that could be distinguished from the group of schizophrenic patients by symptomatology and prognosis.

The possibilities of improving the treatment of depression in the context of general health care are being explored in the framework of a broader investigation of the possibility of introducing mental health components into primary health care services (Harding, 1977). This study is being carried out in seven developing countries: Brazil, Colombia, Egypt, India, the Philippines, Senegal, and Sudan. A baseline investigation of morbidity and services in the catchment areas of the centres has been completed and is now being followed by designing methods of training for specific tasks to be carried out by general health service personnel. After a certain period, during which such tasks will be performed in the general health services, a second evaluation of the mental health situation in the area will be undertaken to assess the effect of the training and organizational intervention.

Simultaneously with these studies on diagnosis, assessment, and classification, WHO has initiated and is coordinating collaborative research on the biological aspects of depressive disorders. Research centres in developed and developing countries are cooperating in projects dealing with the biochemistry, psychopharmacology, and genetics of depression. Thus, for example, the effects of antidepressive drugs are being assessed in a series of patients in different sociocultural and climatic settings (Sartorius, 1973; Vartanian, 1976). This investigation stemmed from observations that there seemed to be differences in the responses to specific medicaments of groups of people from different ethnic groups, and differences in the doses needed to achieve a beneficial response between countries that differ in climate and in the nutritional status and other characteristics of patients. Also under WHO sponsorship, a number of centres are collaborating in studies on genetic aspects and biochemical mechanisms of depressive disorders (Coppen et al., 1977; Gershon et al., 1980) and adding to our store of knowledge by using the advanced laboratory and clinical facilities existing in leading research institutions in the world.

The study described in this report was conceived in 1970 with the collaboration of research centres in Canada (Douglas Hospital and the

Department of Psychiatry in the Montreal General Hospital), Iran (Department of Psychiatry, University of Teheran), Japan (Department of Neuropsychiatry, Nagasaki University School of Medicine, Nagasaki, and Department of Neurology and Psychiatry, Jikei University School of Medicine, Tokyo), and Switzerland (University Psychiatric Clinic, Basle). The first meeting of the collaborating investigators from all the centres took place in early 1972 and, following preparatory work, data collection began later in the same year.

As in other WHO-coordinated research, this study has to contribute to three goals: first, to strengthen the research capacity of centres collaborating in research on problems of public health importance; second, to develop further the methods and instruments needed to study such problems; and third, to make a contribution to knowledge.

More specifically, the project set out to achieve the following objectives:

(a) To develop and test simple instruments for clinical description of depressive states; the instruments should be easy to learn and apply, and at the same time sufficiently standardized to allow cross-cultural comparisons to be made;

(b) To examine with such instruments series of "average" depressive patients in different cultures, selected among those consulting psychiatrists; and

(c) To set up in this process a network of field research centres that would then be capable of initiating epidemiological and follow-up studies, therapeutic trials, and other investigations, as well as providing training to other investigators interested in adopting the same approach.

The report summarizes the experiences of the field investigators and WHO staff collaborating in the first phase of the study, during which methods and instruments were developed, training procedures implemented, and patients selected and assessed in the five research centres.

In the later phases of the project the investigators carried out a follow-up study in which the patients were re-evaluated five years after the initial assessment. In addition, the field research centres undertook studies aimed at determining the proportion of patients with depressive orders among all people attending general health services, and assessing their clinical and social characteristics. The results of these studies and the reviews[1] of the epidemiological literature and rating scales for depression will be published separately.

The instruments developed in the course of the WHO studies have already found wider applications, for example, in assessing the effects of treatment (Reisby et al., 1977; Takahashi et al., 1979), epidemiological surveys (Jablensky et al., 1981), and general practice research (Katschnig et al., 1980). Teams of investigators in other countries (Bulgaria, Federal Republic of Germany, Ghana, India, and Poland) have undertaken clinical, service-oriented, and epidemiological studies utilizing the methodological tools first tested in the five research centres listed above.

Depression is an area of research in which important results can be expected in the not very distant future, leading to improved methods for

---

[1] Prepared as background documents for the project by Dr F. Fenton (Montreal).

prevention and treatment. Different approaches—epidemiological, clinical, biological, and psychosocial—are likely to contribute jointly to this goal, but a prerequisite for their effective integration is the much needed "common language" in the description of depressive states and their classification (Kendell, 1976; Lehmann, 1977). The collaborative efforts of the investigators in the present study, sustained over a number of years, will be amply rewarded if the results of this investigation prove to be a step towards the establishment of an internationally used set of concepts for eliciting and describing clinical findings in depression.

1. Objectives, design, and instrumentation of the study

Objectives

The objectives of the initial assessment phase of the project, whose results are being presented in this report, were:

(*a*) To select suitable study areas and collaborating institutions in several countries that differ from each other with regard to culture, patterns of socioeconomic development, types and methods of operation of the health services, and psychiatric tradition;

(*b*) To develop standardized instruments and procedures for the selection and assessment of patients with depressive disorders from among all those seeking psychiatric care;

(*c*) To train psychiatrists at the collaborating centres to use the instruments developed for the study in a reliable and uniform manner;

(*d*) To assess, with the help of these instruments, series of patients suffering from depressive conditions and to compare their characteristics across the centres.

The achievement of these objectives was intended to establish a baseline for the subsequent part of the project, which was to investigate the course and outcome of depression in different cultures, assess its social consequences, describe the various approaches to its treatment and management, and extend case-finding for depressive conditions into general health services. The latter would not only provide information about the number and types of depressive conditions reaching general health services and about the treatment they receive but would also create a basis for research leading to their better management (Sartorius et al., 1980).

Study areas and facilities

The five selected study areas present interesting demographic, cultural, and social differences that are discussed in detail in Chapter 2. One of them is in a developing country (Iran) where the psychiatric facility chosen for the study has to deal with patients of extremely varied socioeconomic and educational background. The study area in Canada is characterized by its multi-ethnic composition and high social and geographic mobility. The area selected in Switzerland is an urban community with a high proportion of elderly people and relative economic and social stability. The two study areas in Japan contrast in some respects: one (Tokyo) is a vast urban agglomeration and the other (Nagasaki) includes a proportion of rural population and is more traditional in its organization and way of life.

The selection of study areas, however, was by no means intended to be representative of the variety of socioeconomic and cultural conditions in developing and developed countries: attempts to link the findings of the study to specific social, economic, or cultural variables should therefore be seen mainly as efforts to generate hypotheses for future work.

In selecting the study areas, previous findings, public health considerations, and certain hypotheses about depressive disorders (such as the often quoted absence of guilt in patients in Japan, the importance of depression in higher age, and the influence of religion) were taken into account as well as the presence in these areas of teams of investigators who had carried out important previous work on depression and were willing to collaborate in developing new methods of assessing depressive conditions that would allow international comparisons.

Each field research centre was located at a psychiatric treatment facility—a hospital or university clinic—that could be expected to admit a sufficiently large number of depressive patients to make the selection of a study population possible. For the purposes of the project, each centre was requested to delineate a catchment area. The size of the catchment area varied, but as a general rule it encompassed the city in which the centre was located and the surrounding countryside up to a radius of 80 km.

Selection of patients for the study

It was agreed to include in the study all patients residing or sleeping in the catchment area for at least six months prior to the beginning of data collection, provided that they met a number of criteria that strongly indicated that they were suffering from a depressive illness not attributable to cerebral damage, senile brain disease, or toxic disorder. The diagnostic classification of eligible patients (e.g., "endogenous", "reactive", "psychotic" or "nonpsychotic") was not taken into consideration at that stage of selection; a sufficient condition for inclusion was the presence of depressive symptoms in the absence of clear indications of other functional or organic psychiatric illness. Supplementary criteria were specified to exclude patients who would be·difficult to assess by the ordinary methods of clinical investigation (history taking, mental state examination) because of either severely subnormal intelligence or marked sensory defects.

Thus, the criteria for the selection of patients for the study in all the centres were as follows:

Criterion	Rationale
(1) *Age 10–70 years*	To include the entire lifetime risk period for depressive disorders.
(2) *Absence of definite physical disease, toxic disorder, or cerebral damage or disease*	To exclude depressive conditions of an organic origin where treatment and prognosis are determined primarily by the underlying disease.
(3) *Normal intelligence (IQ 70 or higher)*	To exclude patients with whom it would be difficult to carry out a full clinical interview, and patients whose mental subnormality rather than the depression would in the long run determine their management and the outcome.
(4) *Absence of severe language or hearing difficulties*	To exclude patients difficult to interview.
(5) *Absence of psychopathological symptoms indicative of schizophrenia or other non-affective functional psychosis*	To exclude schizophrenia, paranoid psychosis, and reactive psychoses other than depressive, even if accompanied by some depressive symptoms. For example, thought withdrawal, intrusion, and echo of thoughts; delusions or hallucinations not based on a depressed mood would exclude the patient from the study.
(6) *Presence of at least two of the following symptoms: depressive mood, feeling of worthlessness, hopelessness, hypochondriasis, anxiety, suicidal thoughts, feeling of diminution of abilities, self-reproach or guilt, inability to feel or enjoy.*	To include patients who were most likely to be suffering from depressive illness.

These criteria were applied in a screening procedure (see Screen Form, Annex 2), that assessed consecutive admissions or attendances at the facility and selected patients who satisfied the conditions for inclusion.

Development of instruments

Two instruments were developed for the study, a screen form for selecting patients, and a schedule for the standardized recording of data obtained in their clinical assessment.

The screen form (see Annex 2) is a simple checklist of the inclusion/ exclusion criteria described above. The presence of any of the exclusion categories—physical disease, toxic disorder or cerebral damage or disease; severe mental retardation; clear-cut schizophrenic or paranoid psychotic symptoms; severe language or hearing disabilities—would automatically disqualify the patient from the study and at least two of the inclusion categories (symptoms of depression) had to be present to make the patient eligible for the project. In the course of the study, the screen form was tested for specificity and sensitivity; the results are reported in Chapter 3. In principle, the screen form can be applied by a psychiatrist, a general practitioner, or a clinical psychologist familiar with the symptoms of depressive disorders, organic brain disease, schizophrenia, and other functional psychoses. For this study the screen was applied to all patients contacting specified facilities, and satisfying the age and residence criteria.

The Schedule for Standardized Assessment of Depressive Disorders (WHO/SADD), which was the main instrument of the study, was developed keeping the following needs in mind:

(1) The need for a relatively simple instrument, the application and completion of which would take as little time as possible;

(2) The need for an instrument that would allow a comprehensive assessment in the sense that all clinically relevant manifestations of depressive syndromes, as well as essential information on past history, could be rated;

(3) The need for an instrument with cross-cultural applicability, i.e., capable of recording culture-specific characteristics of depressive disorders, including those that could not be predicted from available knowledge;

(4) The need for an instrument composed of items of standardized content accompanied by rating rules so that the schedule could be used for comparative studies;

(5) The need for an instrument that would appeal to clinicians and researchers and serve as a guide for an examination that was acceptable to patients.

To satisfy requirements 1 and 5 it was decided not to prescribe a rigidly structured clinical interview with specified questions, probes, etc., but rather to make a checklist of demographic, past-history, symptomatological and other items to be rated on the basis of the investigator's clinical judgment in a normal diagnostic or follow-up interview. Here and throughout the schedule the investigators were encouraged to use all available information—from the interview, case notes, informants, and other sources. To meet requirement 2, the items were selected by taking into consideration the literature on the phenomenology of depressive disorders, and the experience of the collaborating investigators and other experts. The result was a set of items on which investigators from different schools of psychiatric thinking would be expected to agree as regards their relevance to the assessment of depression. With regard to 3, as distinct from other instruments for the standardized clinical assessment of patients (e.g., the Present State Examination, which was developed through reduction and condensation from a large number of original items), WHO/SADD was drafted as a "core" set of items to which others, including culture-specific open-ended items, could be added.

The rating of these open-ended items for "other symptoms" was to be accompanied by a descriptive note of where such symptoms occurred. Standardization of item content and uniformity of rating (requirement 4) was achieved by supplementing the schedule with a glossary of definitions (to which illustrative questions and probes used in the clinical examination in the different centres were added later) and by defining the rules for making particular ratings on the individual items.

With these characteristics, the schedule was expected to be easy to master and to adapt to a variety of individual interviewing styles. In the course of the study, it underwent a number of modifications, which took into account field experience and were agreed upon by the investigators. The latest, fifth, draft of the instrument is reproduced in Annex 3. It should be noted that some of the results reported in subsequent chapters of this volume were obtained with the earlier, fourth, draft of SADD; where relevant, the differences between the earlier and the latest draft are indicated in the text.

The structure of the schedule (fourth draft) is as follows: Part 1 contains data on the patient and the investigator(s) who completed the schedule, on the interview, and on other sources of information that were used. The data on the patient included name (optional), age and sex, marital status, socioeconomic status, employment, education, religion, and current treatment status. Part 2 is a list of symptoms and signs that can be assessed in a clinical interview and from information provided by informants and other sources, such as case notes. The first section of Part 2 is a checklist of 39 symptoms and signs, common in depressive disorders and defined in the glossary accompanying the schedule. The ratings on these symptoms and signs are made in relation to: (a) the time when the symptom or sign was present (either in the week preceding the interview or at any time during the current episode of illness except that week); (b) the intensity or degree of manifestation of the symptom (absent, mild or severe, occasionally, or continuously present). The checklist also includes open-ended items that allow the recording of rare or culture-specific symptoms. The second section of Part 2 consists of 18 items related to the past history of the patient—for example, number of past episodes, presence of precipitating factors, presence of mental disorder in relatives. Part 3 contains items for recording the diagnosis, an impression of the severity of the condition, and a classification of the patient's diagnosis. In each case, the investigator was requested to make a diagnosis in terms that he would customarily use in his own practice. In addition he was asked to "translate" his diagnosis into a category of the International Classification of Diseases (ICD), Eighth

Revision.[1] To obtain information about the differences and similarities of local variations in the classification of depressive disorders, the categories used at the University Psychiatric Hospital at Basle and at the University Department of Psychiatry in Teheran were also listed in Part 3 of the schedule, and the investigators were asked to classify each patient according to these schemata as well (glossaries were supplied). Also in Part 3 the investigator was required to rate the severity of the condition, to specify the clinical syndrome in addition to the nosological diagnosis, and to indicate the five most important items (symptoms or history data) that he considered to be the reasons for selecting a particular diagnostic category.[2]

Translation of the instruments

The screen form and Schedule for Standardized Assessment of Depressive Disorders (Annexes 2 and 3) were drafted in English and translated into German, Japanese, and Farsi[3] by psychiatrists working with professional translators. The translated version in each of these languages was translated back into English by a person who had not taken part in the first translation and was not familiar with the original. The back-translations were sent to the headquarters of the study, where they were compared with the original. Any divergences of the back-translation from the original were communicated to the field research centre along with comments on their semantic implications. Modifications in the local translation were made accordingly, with repeated back-translation into English, until satisfactory equivalence with the original was attained.

Training in the use of the WHO/SADD schedule

In addition to becoming familiar with the WHO/SADD schedule through trial use, the centres set up certain standard training procedures aimed at ensuring uniform and comparable application. Each field research centre, in the course of the preparation for the data collection phase of the study, produced several films or videotapes of interviews with depressive patients based on the WHO/SADD schedule. They were prepared in the local languages and used extensively in the training of raters; in addition, several of these recordings were used in inter-centre training and reliability exercises. For the reliability exercises they were at first either dubbed in English or supplied with an English transcript. Dubbing was abandoned because of the difficulty of achieving correspondence between the patient's observable expression and psychomotor behaviour and the dubbing reader's tone and inflexion of voice; and only

---

[1] In the latest, fifth, draft of the schedule, the diagnosis is coded in accordance with the Ninth Revision of ICD. In this connexion, see also *Mental disorders: glossary and guide to their classification in accordance with the Ninth Revision of the International Classification of Diseases*, WHO, Geneva, 1978.

[2] These items are not reported in the present publication but are available on request.

[3] Subsequently, research centres in several other countries have adopted the WHO/SADD for use in clinical and epidemiological studies on depression: it is now available also in Bulgarian, French, Hindi, and Polish.

videotapes made originally in English were used as inter-centre exercises. Later in the project audiotapes were added to the training tools.

In addition to films and tapes, each centre prepared five detailed case histories which were used for discussion during the meetings of collaborating investigators and for reliability exercises.

Before data collection began, each investigator had completed at least 10 assessments of patients with WHO/SADD. When new investigators joined the project they were fully trained by experienced users of the schedule and had to carry out at least 10 interviews under supervision before beginning to assess patients independently.

Assessment of the reliability of psychiatric rating

To assess the within-centre reliability of the rating procedure based on WHO/SADD, the investigators in each centre were required to carry out at least 15 joint assessments of patients. Usually two investigators took part, one of whom conducted the interview (in the local language) and made his own ratings while the other observed and listened and made his own independent ratings; the two exchanged roles in the course of the series of assessments so that each had some "active" and some "passive" participations in joint rating procedures. When each interview was completed, they compared their ratings and discussed any disagreements that had arisen (without changing the original ratings), referring to the glossary where necessary. The completed schedules were sent to the study headquarters for a statistical analysis.

The spacing of the reliability exercises varied according to local conditions; however, in each centre five to eight reliability assessments preceded the start of the data collection, and the remainder took place during the assessment of series of patients.

The assessment of reliability across the centres proved to be much more complicated than anticipated because of: (1) the need to use films or videotapes of interviews in English (when even minor differences in comprehension between the raters would tend to lower the agreement); (2) the need for the observers to attune their attention and perception to the interviewing style of the psychiatrist who conducted the filmed or videotaped interview; and (3) the impossibility of cross-questioning or obtaining feedback. Despite such limitations, reliability exercises with films or tapes took place at every meeting and exchange of visits of investigators. In addition to joint ratings at such meetings, several films and videotapes produced in the different centres were circulated to all the investigators, who could view them repeatedly and make ratings under more relaxed conditions.

Coordination of the study

Steps were taken from the start to ensure: (a) the central coordination of instrument and design development, of data storage, and of data processing and analysis; (b) regular meetings and communication between all participants in the study.

Central coordination was achieved by the office of the principal investigator of the project and by designating the WHO Division of Mental Health (then the Mental Health Unit) in Geneva the study headquarters. In addition to helping directly with developing methods, including instruments and design, the principal investigator and other WHO staff took on the responsibility for organizing meetings and exchanges of visits, circulating drafts of instruments and glossaries, etc., and supervising the observance of agreed timetables for completing various activities.

Throughout the study, the investigators maintained communication with one another by means of exchanges of visits arranged to take place at each centre. All aspects of the progress of the study were reviewed during these visits, and the opportunity was also used to do reliability exercises. These exchanges of visits were of unique value also because of the possibility they offered to investigators from different countries to become familiar with other cultures and patterns of mental health care, as well as to see patients in hospital or in their homes.

In conclusion, it is worth pointing out that the costs of designing, implementing, and coordinating the study were modest by any standard. The unabated enthusiasm and motivation of the investigators and the readiness of centres to put aside resources for the study were among the main factors that sustained the project over several years.

2. Research setting: characteristics of the five study areas

The cross-cultural context of the present study offered a rare opportunity to explore and describe the manifestations of a mental disorder in different, even contrasting, cultural and social settings. An additional advantage was that in one of the countries (Japan) two research centres took part in the study and assessed patients from the same "macro-cultural" environment but living, one group, in a large, densely populated city and, the other, in a mixed urban-rural area.

The collection of data on the environment in which particular forms of depression occur, as well as on how such disorders are perceived in the different settings by trained observers sharing a common frame of reference, may contribute to the better understanding of the relation between social and cultural factors and the manifestations of depressive disorders.

Although a systematic investigation of such relations was not feasible in the present study, the investigators collected, as far as possible, data describing the economic, social, and cultural characteristics of the study areas to illustrate the background of the patients who were selected and assessed. Table 1 presents a selection of such data. The data can serve only to illustrate the background to the work of the field research centres in the initial phase of the study. Strict comparisons are not possible because of the many limitations inherent in the data (e.g., origin in different census years, variation in the definitions employed in the census, etc.).

Basle

The canton Basle-City (Basel-Stadt) is situated along the river Rhine in the north-west of Switzerland, and borders on the Federal Republic of Germany and France. The area of the canton is about 37 km² and the density of the population is 6071 per km².

Table 1. Comparisons between selected characteristics of the five catchment areas (data provided by the field research centres)

Selected characteristics	Basle	Montreal	Nagasaki	Teheran	Tokyo
(A) *Geographical and demographic characteristics*					
(1) Area (km^2)	37	2 673	4 069	25 434	17 164
(2) Population	224 630	2 802 480	1 570 000	3 492 500	25 647 067
(3) Population density per km^2	6 071	1 027	383	111	1 494
(4) Percentage rural population	0	0	41	12.5	18
(5) Percentage population aged 0–14	16.3	27.4	28	46	24.3
(6) Percentage population aged 60+	22.1	11.0	12	6	12.3
(7) Birth rate per 1000	10.1	12.3	not available	36.8	20.1
(8) Infant mortality per 1000 live births	15.4	17.0	15.2	120	10.6
(9) Deaths in age group 60+ as percentage of all deaths	83.8	69.9	71.5	not available	71.8
(10) Deaths due to cancer, cardiovascular, and cerebrovascular disease as percentage of all deaths	68.2	71.9	52.8	22	57.2
(11) Suicide rates per 100 000	31	12.1	15.4	2.1	15.3
(12) Percentage households with five or more members	7.7	41.7 (4+ members)	33	39	27.2
(13) Percentage of one-person households	29.3	14.9	9	5.5	18.3
(14) Minorities exceeding 5% of population	Italians data not available	Greeks and Italians data not available	none	none	none
(15) Percentage of population age 7+ with no schooling		data not available	1.6	73.1	0.38

(B) *Health services*

(1) Hospital beds per 1000	15.8	8.1	12.2	data not available	8.49
(2) Psychiatric beds per 1000	2.8	3.3	3.9	0.6	1.74
(3) Number of physicians per 1000	1.46	1.1	1.33	0.2	1.51
(4) Number of psychiatrists	94	335	104	96	2 170
(5) Year when first psychiatric facility established	1842	1875	1913	1920	1879
(6) Year when first psychiatrist started work in area	1861	1875	1907	1937	1879
(7) Annual number of admissions (including readmissions) to psychiatric facilities in area	2 154	9 056	data not available	18 000	60 250
(8) Average length of stay in facilities of centre (days)	data not available	25[a]	150	30	60
(9) Percentage of all admitted patients:					
(a) All psychoses	47.9	43.3	69	84.4	84
(b) Schizophrenia	21	20.3	46	52.3	20.8
(c) Affective psychoses	16.9	11.8	2	23.5	21.2
(d) All neuroses	9.1	20.6	2	7.6	14.3
(e) Alcohol dependence	13.6	18.2	6	0.1	4
(f) Drug dependence	6.8	1.7	less than 1	0.9	1
(g) Other diagnoses	21.1	16.2	22	6.8	38.7

[a] Average length for the hospital's facilities not calculated.

Basel-Stadt is almost exclusively an urban canton. Demographically, the city population is stationary. There is some out-migration of mainly middle-class and particularly younger families with children, while less affluent social groups from the rest of Switzerland and abroad are attracted by the good income opportunities and social services in the canton.

The catchment area of the University Psychiatric Clinic coincides with the canton Basel-Stadt, which includes the communities of Basle (city), Riehen, and Bettingen. Only about 5% of the clinic's patients live outside it.

The population of the canton (1972 census) is 224 627, of which 54% are females and 46% males. Over 22% of the population is aged 60 or more, while the age group 0–14 constitutes less than 15%. The crude birth rate is 10.1 per 1000. Infant mortality is 15.4 per 1000 live births. More than 83% of all deaths occur in the age group over 60; cancer and cardiovascular and cerebrovascular disease are the most important causes of death, accounting together for 68.3% of all deaths.

There are no significant religious or racial minorities in Basle; the population is 53% Protestant and 41% Roman Catholic. However, as ethnic minorities, the foreigners working in Switzerland (especially Italian and Spanish immigrants, who constituted over 17% of the country's population in 1972) present social problems, especially with regard to cultural integration and job security.

Compared with other urban areas in Western Europe the rate of unemployment in Basle is low. Over 51% of the total population is gainfully employed. The principal employers are the services, insurance companies, the banks, and the chemical industry. The last includes, above all, three large pharmaceutical companies that have their research and administration centres in Basle.[1] Agriculture plays no role in the economy of the canton. The service sector provides 56.2% of the employment, compared to 43.9% for Switzerland as a whole. The average income in Basle is in the top range for the whole of Switzerland. The cost of living and especially of housing is also considerably above the national average. The old university and educational tradition of Basle explains also the higher-than-average level of education of the population.

The prevailing family structure is the small nuclear family, composed of parents and one to three children. In 1970, the average size of a household was 2.5 inhabitants. There is a strikingly high proportion of one-person households—29.4% (mainly old people and university students), and a very low proportion (7.7%) of households with five or more members. Most of the people live in flats that have on an average 2.2 rooms and 0.79 inhabitants per room.

The medical services in the area include 11 municipal and private hospitals and the clinics (teaching hospitals) of the University, jointly providing 15.8 hospital beds per 1000 population. The ratio of physicians to population is high: 1.46 per 1000. Excluding psychiatrists, there are 320 practising physicians of all specialties in the city, of which 59 are general practitioners. There are 94 psychiatrists, of whom 28 are in private practice.

---

[1] The production plants have been moved to outside the canton of Basel-Stadt.

The first psychiatric facility in the area was established in 1842. Today the psychiatric services consist of: the University Psychiatric Clinic (600 beds, 1900 admissions per year); the Psychogeriatric Unit Holdenweid (80 beds); the Counselling Service for Alcohol-dependent Persons; the Counselling Service for Drug-dependent Persons; and a private psychiatric clinic, "Sonnenhalde" (63 beds, 222 admissions per year).

The staff of the University Psychiatric Clinic and the outpatient services included 20 service chiefs and supervising physicians, 43 house officers, 10 psychologists, 1 sociologist, 9 social workers, 17 occupational and physical therapists, and 245 nurses.

The University Psychiatric Clinic is the only psychiatric institution obliged to admit patients from the catchment area. Most depressive patients are admitted on a voluntary basis, usually on the advice of the family physician or the family. Compulsory hospitalizations are rare. With very few exceptions, the decision to admit a patient is taken on clinical grounds. There is no selection on the part of the clinic with regard to the patient's financial or general social situation.

The selection of patients for the study in the clinic was made in the special ward for depressive patients according to the general design of the study and the screen form. Shortage of time on the part of the physicians participating in the study was the only reason that not all of the patients were screened. There are no reasons to suspect that this biased the sample in any systematic way.

All study patients were inpatients of the University Clinic of Basle.[1] As a rule the reason for admission was a depressive illness necessitating inpatient treatment. The decision to admit a patient was made on the basis of an evaluation of the suicide risk, the degree of the patient's subjective suffering, and the personal and social situation.

Compared with many other areas the population of the Basle catchment area seems to show greater acceptance of psychiatric hospital care: even patients with mild depression come to the clinic and ask for help. Depressive illnesses of the patients included in the study may therefore be, on the whole, less severe than those of patients admitted to other psychiatric hospitals in the canton or the country. Many newly admitted patients have already been treated with drugs as outpatients either by a general practitioner or by a psychiatrist in private practice.

Montreal (*Catchment area: census metropolitan Montreal area*)

Metropolitan Montreal is 2673 km² in area and has a population of 2 802 480 (1976 census). The catchment area is entirely urban. The population density is 1027 per km². Very few patients living outside this area were included in the study.

The Montreal catchment area is characterized by a rapidly increasing population (between 1966 and 1971 it increased by 6.7%). The crude birth rate

---

[1] Outpatients were not included, because the clinic provides only after-treatment and no primary treatment to outpatients.

is 12.3 per 1000 and the infant mortality rate 17.0 per 1000 live births. The age distribution characterizes the population of the catchment area as being comparatively young: more than 27% are in the age group 0–14 years, and only 11% are above 60. Life expectancy at birth is 69.0 years for males and 76.5 years for females (1977 data). About 70% of all deaths occur in the age group 60+. Cancer and cardiovascular and cerebrovascular disorders are the leading causes of death, accounting between them for 71.9% of all deaths. Accidents and injuries are responsible for 8.7% of all deaths.

The mother tongue of 66.3% of the population is French, and of 21.7% English. About 12% of the population belong to minority groups, mainly Greeks, Italians, Chinese, and Germans. The biggest religious denomination in the area is Roman Catholic.

National census data (1971) indicate that 36.6% of the economically active population are employed in the clerical, sales, and service sectors; 16.9% in management, administration, and the professions; 14.0% in industry and construction; and only 5.9% in agriculture.

The average household size is 3.3 persons. The proportion of one-person households is 14.9%. Of the dwellings in the area, 35.3% are occupied by their owners, and 64.7% by tenants. 50.6% of all dwellings are flats; the rest are houses and a small number (0.1%) are "mobile homes".

Virtually the entire population is covered by the national health insurance plan. The total number of physicians in the area (including general practitioners and specialists) is 3049 or 1.1 per 1000 population; over 70% of the physicians are in private practice.

The ratio of all non-psychiatric beds (acute and chronic) is 8.1 per 1000 population. The psychiatric facilities include eight psychiatric hospitals as well as 20 psychiatric units in general hospitals. The ratio of psychiatric beds to population is 3.3 per 1000 population. The first psychiatric facility in the area was established in 1875.

Two psychiatric facilities took part in the identification and selection of patients for the present study: the Douglas Hospital and the Department of Psychiatry of the Montreal General Hospital.

The Douglas Hospital is the largest English-speaking psychiatric facility in the Province of Quebec; it opened its doors in 1881. Its capacity today is about 900 patients, including 45 children and adolescents. It has responsibility also for 50 patients in family care and for over 2500 outpatients. It admits about 1400 patients annually. Its Community Psychiatric Centre is responsible for the psychiatric care of a catchment area of 250 000 people in the immediate neighbourhood. In addition, all English-speaking psychiatric patients in the Province of Quebec outside of Montreal may be admitted. The medical staff of Douglas Hospital includes 50 psychiatrists and other physicians, 90 consultants, and three dentists. The nursing staff numbers more than 500. Over 500 volunteer workers assist with the care of the patients. Operating funds are provided by the Province of Quebec. The Douglas Hospital is also one of the teaching hospitals in the network of the Department of Psychiatry at McGill University. Its Research Department is best known for its work in clinical psychopathology and psychopharmacology.

The Department of Psychiatry at the Montreal General Hospital, a 900-bed hospital established in 1946, was among the first units of its kind in Canada. From its inception it developed very active clinical services inpatient and outpatient, a day centre, a psychosomatic unit, a behaviour modification unit and, more recently, a night centre.

The Department's catchment area covers a population of approximately 275 000 and comprises three quite diverse areas in metropolitan Montreal: a central "inner city" area; an expanding "suburban" area on the South Shore of the St Lawrence River; and a third area in the east end of Montreal, Traditionally, the Department has served basically an English-speaking or bilingual population. However, more recently, the proportion of French-speaking patients treated in all services has increased. In 1973, 550 patients were admitted to the two inpatient services with 52 beds, for a stay averaging 25 days. The external services include an emergency service, a short-stay intensive care unit, three outpatient clinics (including two "satellite" clinics in the surrounding community), an adolescent service, and an alcoholics programme. In 1973, over 1900 patients were seen in the emergency service. Also, during 1973, an additional 2200 outpatients were treated during the course of about 10 700 treatment contacts.

The total staff in the Department numbers 150, including 38 psychiatrists, and several consulting specialists. Additional professional services are provided by the departments of clinical psychology, social service, and occupational therapy.

A broad spectrum of research activities is being carried out in the Department, including neurochemical and psycho-endocrine research, social and community psychiatry, and psychosomatic research with particular emphasis on the investigation of pain and behaviour modification.

A major characteristic of the metropolitan catchment area is the distinction between population groups on the basis of mother-tongue. While the proportion of bilingual individuals is increasing, it is still usual for French-speaking and English-speaking residents to seek medical care in different services and facilities. Therefore, any series of patients selected for study at a predominantly francophone or predominantly anglophone health facility is bound to be unrepresentative of the area population as a whole, considering the existing cultural differences between the two major language groups. Since the two facilities participating in the present study were predominantly English-speaking, it could be assumed that the patients screened, selected, and assessed were not representative of all those receiving psychiatric care in metropolitan Montreal. On the whole, however, they could be considered as demographically fairly "typical" of the English-speaking segment of the patient population.

Nagasaki (*Catchment area: Nagasaki Prefecture*)

Nagasaki Prefecture, 4096 km^2 in area, occupies the north-western tip of the island of Kyushu. Its diameters are 213 km east to west and 307 km north to south. It is mainly mountainous. The coastline consists of many peninsulas, gulfs, capes, and inlets, and its length reaches 3825 km—the longest in Japan. The annual average temperature is 16.5°C. The population density is 383 per km². Nagasaki Prefecture is a mixed urban-rural area with one big city (Nagasaki) and a surrounding rural area in which about 41% of the population of the prefecture live.

The population of the catchment area (total 1 570 245) is relatively young, 28% being in the age group 0–14 years. The aged (over 60) constitute 12% of the total population. According to 1970 census data, the life expectancy at birth is 69.3 years for males and 74.7 years for females. Infant mortality is 15.2 per 1000 live births (1972 data). About 72% of all deaths occur in the age group 60+, and 52.8% of all deaths are caused by cancer and cardiovascular and cerebrovascular diseases. Accidents and injuries account for 5.3% of all deaths.

Ethnically the population is homogeneous; the percentage of Koreans, Chinese, and other nationalities is negligible.

The three most important sources of occupation in the prefecture are shipbuilding, fishery, and agriculture. More than 47% of the industrial output in the area comes from the shipbuilding industry; the Mitsubishi dockyard in Nagasaki is among the biggest in the world. Fishing is also important and the total catch in Nagasaki Prefecture is among the highest in Japan. The population aged 15 and over is divided by occupation into: farmers and fishermen (including active family members), 17.3%; industrial workers, 17.5%; sales and service employees, 9.4%; various professionals, including engineers, technicians, teachers, and others, 4.4%; administrative and clerical workers, 7.6%; business owners and company executives, 3.8%; students, 9.1%; and housewives, 18.6%. Another 10.8% are not in employment for various reasons. Compared with the national average, the proportion of agricultural workers is high and the proportion of manufacturing workers is low. The average individual income for the Nagasaki Prefecture is around 70% of the figure for Japan as a whole.

The average size of a household in Nagasaki Prefecture is 3.9 persons. About 66% of all families are of the nuclear type. The proportion of one-person households in the area is 9%. Households of six or more members constitute only 9.8% of all households. The average number of rooms per family is 3.8.

Almost all the population is covered by health insurance schemes. The medical and psychiatric services in the area include a total of 157 hospitals (118 general, 31 psychiatric, 7 tuberculosis sanatoria, and 1 isolation hospital for infectious diseases—providing a total of 19 248 beds), 1174 general outpatient clinics, and 408 dental clinics. There are still places in the distant islands where medical services are extremely scarce.

The total number of psychiatric beds is 6165 (or 3.9 per 1000 population). The total number of physicians in the prefecture is 2093 (1.3 per 1000) of whom about 60% are mainly in private practice. There are 104 psychiatrists (0.7 per 10 000) and 1366 nurses employed in the psychiatric services. The first psychiatric facility in the area was established in 1913. In the psychiatric services 92.2% of all beds (in the Nagasaki area) are in private psychiatric hospitals, but in addition there are three public psychiatric hospitals, one psychiatric ward in the National Hospital and one in the University Hospital. Community-oriented activities to promote public mental health in the prefecture are still limited, although there is a prefectural mental health centre. There are not yet institutions comparable to the halfway house.

The Department of Neuropsychiatry of the Nagasaki University Hospital (the field research centre in the study) has an inpatient unit with 48 beds and an outpatient service. The annual number of admissions is about 100, with an average length of stay around 150 days. The outpatient clinic provides services for about 1500 patients (12 000 attendances) per year, of which 30% are first attendances. The staff of the University Psychiatric Unit includes 13 service chiefs and consultants, 16 other psychiatrists, and 17 nurses. In addition to teaching and service activities, the Department is also an active research centre; the main areas of research are psychopharmacology, neurophysiology, biochemistry, and clinical psychiatry.

A comparison of the age distribution of the patients screened for the study and the general population of the prefecture showed minor deviations except for an under-representation among the study population of persons in the age groups 15–19, 25–29, and 30–34. The under-representation of younger age groups (15–34), however, was more marked when the patients selected for inclusion in the study were compared with the general population.

Teheran

The area selected for the study had a population of 3 492 500 in 1966 (census data) and covers a surface with a radius of about 80 km around Teheran. It includes eight towns of more than 5000 inhabitants each and a large number of other small towns and villages. Apart from Teheran, which had a population of 2 719 730 in 1966, the largest towns are Tajrish with 157 489 population, Ray with 102 825, and Karaj with 44 242.

Teheran came into being as an urban settlement and a capital not more than 200 years ago. It has developed quickly during the past 50 years, and now it is a rapidly expanding city. Its present population is certainly much higher than the 1966 census figure. According to preliminary reports from the 1976 census, it had reached 4 496 159 and continued to grow at a rate of 4.2% per year. Teheran is also the principal city of the Central Ostan (province), which has a population of over five million. About 62.1% of the total population of Iran live in rural and 37.9% in urban areas. The corresponding figures for Central Ostan, however, are 29.7% and 70.3%, and for the catchment area 12.6% and 87.4% respectively.

The study area, including the city of Teheran, had a population density of 111.2 persons per km^2 (978.5 per km^2 in Teheran, according to 1966 data). This is well above the average for the country (15.6 per km^2) and for the Central Ostan (54.5 per km^2).

A detailed breakdown of the population by age is not available for the catchment area but some general trends can be illustrated by national figures. Demographically, the population of Iran is very young, 46.1% of the total population being under 15 years of age (52.2% male and 47.8% female). Only 6% are 60 years of age and over. 58.7% of all men and 72.6% of all women aged 10 years and over are married.

The crude birth rate for Iran in 1972 was 36.8 per 1000 population and the crude death rate 4.9 per 1000. Thus the annual natural increase rate is about 32 per 1000. Infant mortality is about 120 per 1000 live births. The proportion of all deaths occurring in the age group 60+ is not known but the proportion occurring in the first 11 months of life is 28.5%. Cancer and cardiovascular and cerebrovascular diseases account for no more than 22% of all deaths; while accidents and injuries contribute 8.8%. The main causes of death are the infectious and respiratory diseases, especially in infancy and early childhood.

In terms of residential mobility, the population of Iran may be divided into a settled population and unsettled or nomadic groups whose movements and residence follow seasonal or occupational changes. The latter groups include the properly nomadic (about 15 per 1000 of the total population) and people who move constantly between villages and towns, such as gypsies and vendors (8 per 1000 of the total population). The unsettled population of the study area is only 1.2 per 1000.

The within-country migration rate is high: about 23% (35% in the Central Ostan). The main reasons for migration include changes of employment, military or civil service duty, marriage, and study. About 60% of the migrants move together with their families.

In 1971, only 36.9% of the population aged six years and over was literate (47.7% males and 25.5% females).

The diversity of the population of Iran is also manifested in the existence of religious minorities who have lived in Iran since ancient times, before the adoption of Islam as a result of the Arab conquest in 641. While Islam is the religion of the majority, there are several religious minorities who live as communities with their own separate identity. Besides Farsi they speak their own language, and at their schools the religion is being taught to the children in their own mother-tongue. These religious minorities include the Zoroastrians (0.08%), the Jews (0.24%), the Armenians (0.43%), the Assyrians (0.08%), other Christian communities (0.08%), and other religions (0.31%).

In 1972, 43.2% of the total population of Iran aged 10 years and over were economically active. Of them, 90.7% were in some kind of employment; 47.5% of the employed group were engaged in agriculture, and 26.5% in industrial and 26% in administrative occupations. The remaining 56.8% economically nonactive population comprised 64.2% housewives, 21.2% students and 14.7% others.

The Iranian family, on average, has four to five members. One-person households constitute 5.5%; large households with six or more members represent 38.8% of all households. The traditional extended family was the prevalent type but in many places, especially in the cities, it is gradually giving way to the nuclear family. Likewise, the old individual houses with rather spacious rooms and courtyards are being replaced by small apartment buildings in large residential blocks.

There are 0.9 physicians for every 10 000 persons, and 0.04 psychiatrists for every 10 000 persons in the whole country. The corresponding figures for Teheran are 2 and 0.2 respectively (1972).

Psychiatric beds represent 8.8% of all hospital beds in Iran; the corresponding figure for Teheran was 10.9% (1966). There is one psychiatric bed per 10 000 inhabitants for the whole country, and 6.0 beds per 10 000 population for Teheran (1972). The total number of psychiatric beds in Iran is 3690 of which 2125 are in Teheran. There were 119 psychiatrists working in Iran, of whom 96 were in Teheran (1972).

Roozbeh Hospital, the field research centre of the present study, is the psychiatric teaching hospital of the University of Teheran and is located in one of the densely populated sectors of Teheran. It admits patients from all parts of Teheran, as well as from the provinces, including remote parts of the country. About 80% of patients are referred from Teheran and 20% from the provinces. This hospital has 100 beds, 80 psychiatric and 20 neurological, and an attached outpatient clinic. The annual number of admissions is about 900 patients and the average length of stay about 30 days. The outpatient clinic has about 11 000 attendances per year, of which 20% are first attendances.

In the absence of demographic data on the population seeking mental health care in Teheran and the surrounding area, it is difficult to estimate whether the patients screened and selected for the study deviate from the general trends. As regards the facility itself, however, there is no reason to expect that the patients with depressive disorders selected for the study were in any way unusual or different from patients suffering from depressive illnesses seeking care at Roozbeh Hospital at any other time in the last decade or so.

Tokyo (*Catchment area: Tokyo Prefecture*)

The area around and including Tokyo city, which consists of four prefectures (Tokyo, Kanagawa, Saitama, Chiba, and part of Ibaragi Prefecture), is approximately in the middle of Japan and is also at the centre of Japanese politics, economy, and culture. The catchment area, Tokyo Prefecture, has a surface of 17 164 km². The network of private and national railways, the motorways and the airports ensure effective communications with the rest of the country. The density of the population (1494 per km²) is the highest in the country.

The area is a plain surrounded by mountains to the north and west. There is little rain or snow in winter, although temperatures are rather low. In summer the weather is humid with a high rainfall. The area is predominantly urban, but 18% of the population are classified as rural.

The population of the catchment area is 25 647 067, over 23% of the population of the country. The very high population density in the catchment area is caused by the concentration of industry, especially in such large cities as Tokyo, Yokohama, and Kawasaki. The proportion of the working population engaged in sectors other than agriculture is very high in Tokyo and Kanagawa Prefectures.

The proportion of the age group 0–14 is 24.3%; those aged 60+ constitute

12.3% of the population. The crude birth rate is about 20 per 1000 population. Almost 72% of all deaths occur in the age group 60+, and cancer and cardiovascular and cerebrovascular diseases account jointly for over 57% of all deaths (accidents and injuries contribute 5.1%). The infant mortality rate is very low: 10.6 per 1000 live births.

The population of Japan is homogeneous and there are no widespread ethnic group problems.

A social problem, which is a left-over from the past, is the low status of the social group called Burakumin; historically, these people belonged to the lowest social stratum and were traditionally engaged in menial jobs that other classes were not supposed to do. However, the number of Burakumin in the catchment area is very small (far less than 1%), and prejudice against them now finds expression only rarely (e.g., in relation to marriage).

The illiteracy rate in the area is only 0.3% (compared with 0.7% for Japan as a whole); the percentage of university graduates in the area is high: 9.9%.

The study area is the biggest industrial region of Japan, producing more than one-third of the nation's industrial output. The main industries in Tokyo are metals, machinery, and chemicals.

The most important agricultural product of the area is rice. Because of industrialization, the pattern of agriculture is somewhat peculiar: intensive farming of vegetables and flowers takes place on plots of farmland remaining among residential areas and factory sites.

Coastal fishing has declined, and the cultivation of seaweed and shellfish in Tokyo Bay is diminishing in importance because of the pollution of the sea due to factory wastes and land reclamation.

With respect to occupations, the proportions of industrial workers and technicians, professionals, managers and officials, and clerical and related workers in the area are higher than the national average, while the proportions of farmers and fishermen are much lower. The average *per capita* income in Tokyo is about 150% of the national average.

An important characteristic of the Tokyo catchment area is the high percentage (17.7%) of one-person households and small nuclear families. The higher percentage of this type of household and family structure in Tokyo is probably a result of the advanced urbanization of the area, small space for living accommodation, and a still serious housing shortage. The average number of rooms per household is 3.3 (3.9 for the country as a whole). There are many public housing projects, which in 1970 provided a total of 197 000 flats (171 000 rented and 26 000 owner-occupied). Many blocks of flats have been built on the outskirts of Tokyo and Yokohama for commuters to these industrial centres. Most of the housing, however, is of a type that makes it difficult for the residents to feel members of an integrated community.

The large population of the catchment area receive health care at 1545 hospitals with a total of 217 947 beds, 17 338 general clinics, and 116 public health centres. Almost everyone is covered by various health insurance schemes; only 0.7% pay direct for medical services. There are 38 922 physicians in the area, of whom 49.4% are engaged primarily or only in private practice.

Mental health care is provided by 145 psychiatric hospitals with a total of 48 159 beds and by four mental health centres, one in each prefecture. However, the public health centres (one for every 100 000 population), among their many responsibilities, have the duty of providing mental health consultations and home visiting to psychiatric patients. The mental health centres maintain a close connexion with these general services, by ensuring consultations, inservice training for staff of the public health centres, and other support services.

The field research centre participating in the present study, the Department of Psychiatry and Neurology of Jikei University Hospital, is located in the centre of Metropolitan Tokyo and has an inpatient and outpatient clinic offering medical services to those psychiatric patients who voluntarily or semivoluntarily come for help. The inpatient clinic has 50 beds, and 200–250 patients are admitted every year for a stay averaging 60 days. At the outpatient clinic 2000–2500 patients are seen and treated each year, of which about 10% are first attendances. The total staff numbers 89, including 38 psychiatrists, 9 postgraduate students and residents, 4 clinical psychologists and 26 nurses.

Such a comparison, even in very general terms, would be extremely difficult because of the vast population and the large number of psychiatric services in the area. As regards the field research centre, however, the types of patient screened and included in the study did not deviate from the average types of patient with depressive illnesses seen at the Department of Psychiatry and Neurology of the Jikei University Hospital.

Considering the high rate of industrialization, urbanization, and social change in Japan, it may be of interest to compare the demographic, social, and economic characteristics of Tokyo as an excessively overpopulated city with those of Nagasaki as a prefecture that is underpopulated because many young people leave it for other prefectures.

In Tokyo, there has been a drastic increase of the population in the post-war period; by contrast, the population of Nagasaki Prefecture has decreased by 4.3% since 1965. Only in Nagasaki City and its suburbs has it increased. Tokyo has a higher proportion of the productive population aged 15–64 years than Nagasaki, which has higher proportions of the population in the 0–14 and over-65 age groups. As a result of the concentration of persons aged 15–64 there is a high proportion of young unmarried males and females in Tokyo, while in Nagasaki this proportion is low. This tendency is reflected in the higher proportion of one-person households in Tokyo.

As regards employment, manufacturing industries provide 30.9% of all employment in the Tokyo area, followed by sales and services, and the construction industry. On the other hand, agriculture is more important in Nagasaki Prefecture. Skilled, semiskilled, and unskilled workers predominate in Tokyo, and farmers, fishermen, and forestry workers in Nagasaki.

Assuming a national standard of 100%, the level of *per capita* income in Tokyo is 150.4% and in Nagasaki 79.1%

Indices of standard of living and "modernity"—such as income, availability of information (books, journals, newspapers, and number of television sets), level of education, level of motorization, and spread of consumer goods for long-term use—are all higher in Tokyo than in Nagasaki. However, as already emphasized, Tokyo is overpopulated and suffers various corresponding disadvantages: the living area *per capita* is extremely small, crime rates are high, and the air is polluted with dust and sulfurous acid droplets that produce photochemical smog. On the whole, the natural environment in Tokyo has deteriorated to a much greater extent than in Nagasaki.

3. Validity of the screening procedure and reliability of the patient assessment

Validity and applicability of the screening procedure

The purpose of the screening procedure that was applied to a series of consecutive inpatients and outpatients in the centres was to differentiate probably depressed patients from others.

The WHO/SADD Screening Form (reproduced in Annex 2) specifies two sets of criteria for use by the psychiatrist to decide whether to include a patient in the study. The first set had four exclusion criteria: (*a*) presence of definite physical disease, toxic disorder, or cerebral damage or disease; (*b*) moderate or severe mental retardation (IQ 70 or less); (*c*) presence of one or more symptoms characteristic of psychoses other than affective, and in particular schizophrenia—thought withdrawal or intrusion, "echo" of thought, delusions of control, elaborate systems of delusions (other than guilt, hypochondriasis, impoverishment, nihilism), elaborate hallucinations with content other than depressive; and (*d*) presence of severe language or hearing difficulties. A patient exhibiting none of these *exclusion* criteria could be considered for inclusion in the main study if at least two of the following eight *inclusion* criteria were present: depressive mood, suicidal thoughts, hopelessness, feelings of worthlessness, hypochondriasis and/or anxiety, feelings of diminution of ability, self-reproach or guilt, and inability to feel or enjoy These inclusion criteria were selected so as to correspond to symptoms of disorders that would be considered depressive by psychiatrists in all the different centres taking part in the study. Symptoms that would distinguish between forms or subtypes of depressive disorders were not included in the screen.

Screening procedure

In all centres, except Teheran, a special test of the screening procedure was carried out independently of the main study. In Teheran, this test took place at the same time as the selection of patients for the main study.

For every patient screened, the psychiatrist's decision to select or not to select the patient for the main study was recorded on the screen form. The clinical diagnosis made at the facility, independently of the screening procedure, was subsequently recorded on the form, for both included and excluded patients. The screening of consecutive admissions and attendances continued until at least 100 patients eligible for the main study had been identified in each centre.

Measures of validity of the screen

The validity of a screening procedure has been defined as "the measure of the frequency with which the results of that test are confirmed by an acceptable diagnostic procedure—i.e., the ability of the test to separate those who have the condition from those who do not" (Wilson & Jungner, 1968).

In the present study, the validity criterion of the screen's capacity to distinguish depressed patients from other kinds of patients was the clinical diagnosis made independently by routine psychiatric assessment.

A perfect screening test should be able to detect all individuals in a defined group or population who have the disorder without giving false-negative or false-positive results. This requirement is related to two measures of validity commonly used to evaluate screening procedures: sensitivity and specificity.

Sensitivity can be defined as the ability of a test to classify as "positive" all those who have the disorder that is being investigated—i.e., it is a measure of the rate of false-negative results of the screening test (the fewer false-negative results, the more sensitive the procedure).

Specificity, by contrast, is the ability of the test to classify as "positive" only those who have the disorder, and none or as few as possible of those who do not have it. Therefore, specificity is a measure of the rate of false-positive results of the screening procedure (the fewer false-positives, the more specific the test).

Sensitivity and specificity can be presented as proportions:

$$\text{Sensitivity} = \frac{\text{Subjects who have the disorder and are classified as "positive" by the test}}{\text{All subjects in the population who have the disorder}} \times 100$$

$$\text{Specificity} = \frac{\text{Subjects who do not have the disorder and are classified as "negative" by the test}}{\text{All subjects in the population who do not have the disorder}} \times 100$$

Sensitivity and validity of the screen for depressive disorders in the different centres

All screen forms with recorded diagnoses were analysed at the study headquarters in the following way: a list of all diagnoses made on the screened

Table 2. Sensitivity and specificity of the screen for depressive disorders by centre

	Basle	Montreal	Nagasaki	Teheran	Tokyo	All centres
Number of patients screened	272	192	210	234	300	1208
Sensitivity (%)	91.2	81.8	78.7	83.3	89.6	85.8
Specificity (%)	91.8	84.1	88.3	93.8	92.6	90.4

series of patients was compiled, and each diagnosis was rated on a 5-point scale according to its estimated "distance" from a nonorganic depressive disorder. For example, a diagnosis of "periodic depression" would be rated as 0, and a rating of 4 would be given to diagnostic categories clearly excluding a depressive disorder of the types to be included in the study (e.g., delirium tremens or senile dementia). A rating of 1 was given to diagnostic categories close to depression or not excluding depression (e.g., hypochondriacal neurosis, anxiety state, etc.). Ratings 2 or 3 were given to diagnostic categories that were distant from a nonorganic depressive illness but·might still be considered in a differential diagnosis (e.g., hebephrenic schizophrenia was rated 3).

In calculating the indices of sensitivity and specificity of the screen, only the group of patients with a clinical diagnosis rated 0 was considered as a criterion group. The results, by centre, are presented in Table 2.

The results indicate that for the total series of 1208 screened patients the sensitivity and specificity of the depression screen were relatively high; 85.8% and 90.4% respectively. Sensitivity appeared to be highest in Basle and Tokyo, where only 8.8% and 10.4% of all patients with confirmed depressive disorders were missed by the screen (false-negatives), and lower in Teheran, Montreal and Nagasaki, where 16.7%, 18.2% and 21.3% respectively were missed. The specificity of the screen was highest in Teheran, Tokyo and Basle, where only 6.2%, 7.4% and 8.2% of all patients passed by the screen had illnesses other than depressive (false-positive), and somewhat lower in Nagasaki and Montreal, where the rate of false-positives was 11.7% and 15.9% respectively.

Since the specificity of the screen was higher than its sensitivity in all centres, it can be concluded that the screening procedure tended to be somewhat under-inclusive—i.e., it selected for the study mainly patients who were likely to be considered depressive by most psychiatrists, and excluded patients in whom a diagnosis of depression might still be considered but would command less agreement.

Reliability of the WHO/SADD assessments

Introduction

Three conditions must be satisfied if data obtained in a cross-cultural study of a psychiatric disorder are to be compared across different settings. Firstly, all relevant dimensions of the disorder should be investigated; therefore, the psychiatric assessment must be structured. Secondly, the items describing the characteristics of the patient's condition should have the same meaning to the different investigators participating in the study; therefore, the data obtained in a clinical interview should be obtained by well-trained investigators who use a glossary and set of instructions on how to record their findings in a standard manner. Thirdly, to achieve comparability of the findings, these characteristics should be assessed reliably both within and among centres.

Notes on the concept of reliability in psychiatry and the techniques of estimating it are given in Annex 1.

Intracentre reliability

To assess the reliability of the rating procedure when the schedule was used in the field research centres a series of rating exercises was carried out. During an exercise the same patient was rated simultaneously by two or more psychiatrists, one of them filling in the schedule while conducting the interview and the other (or others) observing and making independent ratings. The observer(s) was (were) given an opportunity to ask clarifying questions after the end of the interview.

A total of 83 such rating exercises were performed; Table 3 shows the distribution by field research centre.

Four groups of items were distinguished for the assessment of reliability— sociodemographic items, symptoms and signs of the patient's present state, past history items, and diagnostic categories.

For purposes of analysis, some of the items were regrouped. Ratings on symptoms and signs were dichotomized into "present" and "absent" categories by taking ratings 0, "not applicable" and "uncertain", as negative and ratings 1 and 2 as positive. The diagnoses were grouped into three classification categories: (*a*) endogenous depressive illnesses including diagnoses of periodic depression, involutional depression, and circular depression; (*b*) psychogenic depression including diagnoses of exhaustion depression, neurotic depression, and reactive depression; and (*c*) other forms of depression.

The data from all 83 reliability exercises were first analysed together; subsequently individual centre values were calculated.

Sociodemographic items. The values for the sociodemographic variables (all centres combined) are shown in Table A2 (Annex 1). As might be expected, age, sex, and similar categories can be assessed very reliably. The reliability coefficients are all close to 1, with an average of 0.98, except in the instance of ratings of the highest level of education reached. Agreement on that item was lowest in Montreal and Nagasaki (Table A3, Annex 1).

In Nagasaki low values can be explained by insufficient clarity of instruction: for some of the patients one of the rating psychiatrists coded the

Table 3. Number of reliability exercises by centre

	Basle	Montreal	Nagasaki	Teheran	Tokyo	Total
Number of reliability exercises	8	18	20	19	18	83

educational level to be 5–12 completed years of school, even when the information was vague, concluding the length of schooling to have been in the range. In similar cases other psychiatrists would have given the rating "unknown". Without these cases the intraclass correlation coefficient would have been 0.88 and the corresponding transformed value 0.94.

The Symptom Profile. The second part of the schedule refers to the patient's symptoms. Thirty-nine symptoms and signs were to be rated as present/absent during the last week before the interview, and as present/absent at any time before this period. Analyses were first carried out separately to quantify the reliability in assessing symptoms "present during the last week" and "at any time during the episode but before last week".[1] Then both ratings were combined so that a symptom was considered to be present when it was coded 1 or 2 in either of these time intervals. There was no systematic improvement or decrease in the reliability when combining the ratings of "last week" and "any time in the episode". Therefore, only those results of the reliability analyses that refer to the psychiatrists' assessment of the patients' symptoms during the time before the week preceding the interview are shown and discussed here.

The reliability profile, combining the reliability exercises of all centres, showed some surprising results: the delusional items of the checklist (such as delusions of guilt, hypochondriasis, impoverishment, nihilism, and others) showed π-values of 1.00 or 0.99, i.e., indicating higher reliabilities than, for example, marital status (Table 4).

Therefore, it may be useful to look at the frequencies with which the individual symptoms were rated as present in the group of patients in the reliability exercises (Table A4, Annex 1).

Delusions of guilt, hypochondriasis, impoverishment, and other delusions were rated as present in only 0.6% of the patients. The high agreement of the psychiatrists on items concerning delusions is therefore agreement on the symptoms' absence. Hence a π-value of 0.99 signifies that the probability of

Table 4. Symptoms with very high reliability of assessment of absence or presence

Symptom	π^a	φ^b
1. Sadness	0.99	0.84
21. Delusions of hypochondriasis	0.99^c	0.61
22. Delusions of impoverishment	0.99^c	0.61
23. Other delusions	0.99^c	—
12. Loss of ability to concentrate	0.98	0.83
20. Delusions of guilt	0.96^c	0.34

^{a} π = is the solution of $a = \pi^2 + (1 - \pi)^2$ where a is the agreement ratio.
^{b} $\varphi = \sqrt{\chi^2/N}$ (N = total number of ratings).
^{c} Agreement on absence of the symptom.

---

[1] The 5th Revision of the schedule has been changed in the light of experience and these results: there are now two ratings, one to cover the last month and the other to cover the whole of the present episode (see Annex 3).

agreeing on absence when the symptom is absent is very high. On the other hand, on the basis of the data available, nothing can be said about the probability of "correctly" assessing the presence of a delusional symptom. Similarly, sadness was rated as present in more than 90% of the patients in the reliability exercise. The high π-value for this symptom, therefore, reflects mainly the reliability of "correctly" rating the item as present. For most of the other symptoms and signs in the schedule there was sufficient variation to interpret π as the average probability in assessing the symptoms "correctly", both when symptoms were present and when symptoms were absent.

It should be noted that a low φ-value in this context does not necessarily mean low reliability, since the actual agreement between the raters was almost complete. In the series of patients examined in reliability exercises, however, there were very few in whom delusions were present. The rarity of any item (delusional symptoms in this instance) tends to lower the value of reliability coefficients, like the φ-value, which assesses *both* agreement on absence and agreement on presence of the item. This is not the case with the π-value, for which *separate* values can be computed for presence and absence of a given item.

The reliability profile for all centres combined is indicated in Fig. 1. The confidence intervals for a confidence level of 95% are also shown. In this diagram reliability is expressed in terms of the probabilities π. The average of all the 39 π-values is 0.96 which corresponds to an average agreement ratio of 0.92. None of the symptoms has a π-value less than 0.90 and only ten symptoms were assessed with a reliability less than or equal to 0.94.[1] In Table A5 (Annex 1) only those symptoms are listed for which, in the sample of reliability exercises, at least 20% but not more than 80% of the scores were marked either present or absent. For items marked present or absent in more than 80% of the ratings the reliability was very high. But, as already discussed, in such situations the interpretation of the reliability is restricted to assessing absence (or presence) of symptoms.

Table A5 (Annex 1) also gives the reliability profiles for symptomatology in terms of π separately for each centre. Basle, with only eight patients in the reliability exercises, shows the greatest variation, with considerable difficulties in rating psychomotor agitation ($\pi = 0.5$). The symptoms slowness of thought, indecisiveness, loss of interest, ideas of persecution, delusions of guilt, psychomotor retardation and constipation have π-values less than 0.90. The other centres show patterns similar to the overall profile. Again, in Teheran, additional training of the raters resulted in an increased reliability with an average π-value of 0.99 (see Table 5).

Table 5. Average π-values by centres based on symptom items (only symptoms coded as present in 20% to 80% for the ratings)

	Basle	Montreal	Nagasaki	Teheran	Tokyo	Total
All symptoms	0.93	0.96	0.97	0.99	0.93	0.96

---

[1] It should be noted that the confidence interval is not symmetrical about the estimated π value.

Fig. 1. Reliability: Intracentre—all centres combined—for each (number coded) symptom or sign. Reliability coefficients are indicated with lower and upper confidence limits (95%)

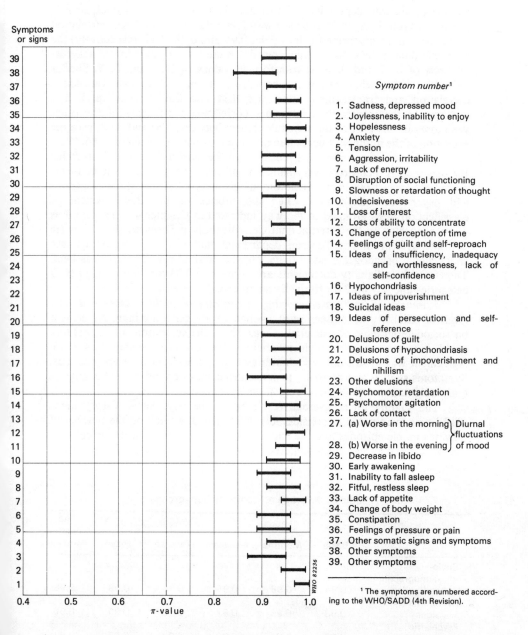

Symptoms or signs

Symptom number[1]

1. Sadness, depressed mood
2. Joylessness, inability to enjoy
3. Hopelessness
4. Anxiety
5. Tension
6. Aggression, irritability
7. Lack of energy
8. Disruption of social functioning
9. Slowness or retardation of thought
10. Indecisiveness
11. Loss of interest
12. Loss of ability to concentrate
13. Change of perception of time
14. Feelings of guilt and self-reproach
15. Ideas of insufficiency, inadequacy and worthlessness, lack of self-confidence
16. Hypochondriasis
17. Ideas of impoverishment
18. Suicidal ideas
19. Ideas of persecution and self-reference
20. Delusions of guilt
21. Delusions of hypochondriasis
22. Delusions of impoverishment and nihilism
23. Other delusions
24. Psychomotor retardation
25. Psychomotor agitation
26. Lack of contact
27. (a) Worse in the morning ⎫ Diurnal
    ⎬ fluctuations
28. (b) Worse in the evening ⎭ of mood
29. Decrease in libido
30. Early awakening
31. Inability to fall asleep
32. Fitful, restless sleep
33. Lack of appetite
34. Change of body weight
35. Constipation
36. Feelings of pressure or pain
37. Other somatic signs and symptoms
38. Other symptoms
39. Other symptoms

[1] The symptoms are numbered according to the WHO/SADD (4th Revision).

π-value

WHO 82236

Items describing past history. The reliability profile for items describing a patient's psychiatric history is plotted in Fig. 2. The average π-value for all the 18 items combined is 0.91.

However, there is considerable variation within the categories. While the number of previous depressive episodes and the number of years since the first depressive episode could be assessed with high reliability (intraclass correlation coefficients and transformed values 0.96, 0.95 and 0.98, 0.97, respectively) the corresponding values for manic episodes were rather low: intraclass correlations of 0.37 and 0.54 or transformed values of 0.68 and 0.77. Similar difficulties arose when rating the course of the present episode (intraclass correlation and transformed values are 0.34 and 0.67, respectively). The π-values or the transformed intraclass correlation coefficients of the other symptoms in this part of the schedule ranged between 0.90 and 0.98, with the exception of the number of years free of symptoms with a π-value of 0.86.

Diagnostic categories. The reliability of the part of the schedule in which the diagnosis is recorded is very similar in all the centres. There was complete agreement ($\pi = 1.00$) in the dichotomous distinction between the endogenous and psychogenic depression when the rubrics of the Basle system of classification were grouped in the way indicated in Chapter 4. The diagnoses given according to the International Classification of Diseases (ICD) system and the system of the Teheran department had not been regrouped into endogenous, psychogenic and others, but the original classification was kept. Therefore, the reliability coefficients are lower: $\pi = 0.93$ for the four-digit ICD categories and $\pi = 0.82$ for the Teheran diagnostic system.

Summary of findings concerning intracentre reliability assessment. The levels of reliability in intracentre assessments were generally high. Agreement on sociodemographic characteristics was 98%. The symptoms and signs, too, could be assessed with high reliability. The average π-value was 0.96. Agreement was lowest on hypochondriasis and assessment of sleep problems. Symptoms such as loss of ability to concentrate, lack of appetite, and change of body weight, at $\pi = 0.98$ each, were at the upper end.

The slightly lower average reliability of the psychiatric history items (91%) was mainly due to considerable difficulties in estimating the number of previous manic episodes and the number of years since the first manic episode. Similar difficulties were encountered in assessing the course of the present episode. Table 6 summarizes the results.

Table 6. Average reliability by item groups

	Basle	Montreal	Nagasaki	Teheran	Tokyo	All centres combined
1. Socio-demographic categories	0.94	0.98	0.95	0.99	0.99	0.98
2. Symptoms and signs	0.93	0.96	0.97	0.99	0.93	0.96
3. Psychiatric history	0.98	0.90	0.90	0.99	0.95	0.91

Fig. 2. Intracentre reliability—psychiatric history items with π-values (items 40–49, 56) and intraclass correlation coefficients (items 50–55, 57, 58) transformed to the range 0.5–1.0 showing lower and upper confidence limits (95%)

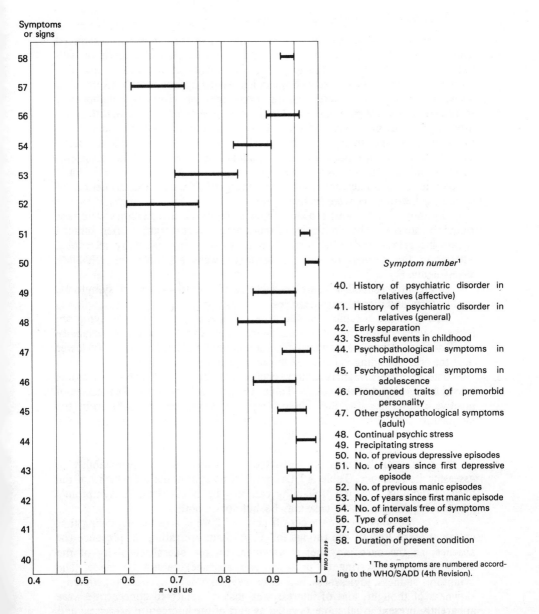

Symptom number[1]

40. History of psychiatric disorder in relatives (affective)
41. History of psychiatric disorder in relatives (general)
42. Early separation
43. Stressful events in childhood
44. Psychopathological symptoms in childhood
45. Psychopathological symptoms in adolescence
46. Pronounced traits of premorbid personality
47. Other psychopathological symptoms (adult)
48. Continual psychic stress
49. Precipitating stress
50. No. of previous depressive episodes
51. No. of years since first depressive episode
52. No. of previous manic episodes
53. No. of years since first manic episode
54. No. of intervals free of symptoms
56. Type of onset
57. Course of episode
58. Duration of present condition

[1] The symptoms are numbered according to the WHO/SADD (4th Revision).

When agreement on diagnosis is assessed by classifying diagnoses into categories of endogenous and psychogenic depression and other diagnoses, coefficient values are 1.00. For specific ICD diagnostic rubrics reliability coefficients of 85–95% were found.

Results of intercentre reliability assessment

Intercentre agreement in assessing depressive disorders was examined using results of joint ratings of live and recorded clinical interviews with patients. Ten films (or videotapes) were produced in the centres for this purpose. The interviews were in English and lasted approximately 45 minutes. These recordings were rated during exchanges of visits of collaborating investigators and by circulating material among the centres. Several difficulties arose in this part of the study. First, interviews had to be conducted in English, the only language spoken by all investigators. This meant that in Basle, Teheran and Tokyo, English-speaking patients had to be found. The recordings had to be assessed by raters whose mother-tongue was not English, on the basis of interviews conducted in English by psychiatrists with patients, neither of whose mother-tongues were English.

Secondly, for obvious reasons, tapes rated by all investigators were best suited for analyses: the circulation of tapes across vast distances often entailed significant delays and difficulties. Two tapes were not rated by all raters. Therefore, the ratings of only eight tapes were available for reliability assessments.

Intercentre reliability exercises were restricted to ratings of symptoms, past history, and diagnostic categories.

In Fig. 3 the reliability profile in terms of π is plotted for the symptom items together with the 95% confidence intervals. The average reliability coefficient is 0.88 with a standard deviation of 0.07 and hence about 10% lower than the corresponding value in the intracentre analysis.

The extremely high reliability coefficients for the delusional symptoms must be interpreted with caution. Table A6 (Annex 1) gives the frequencies of positive ratings for the individual symptoms based on the data from the intercentre reliability exercises. It is obvious that for some symptoms the variability of the scores is quite limited, e.g., sadness was scored positive in 96% of all ratings. Therefore any statement on this symptom's reliability based on the data available must be restricted to a statement on the reliability of assessing its presence. Table A7 (Annex 1) lists symptoms for which, on the basis of the data available, reliability can only be assessed on the symptom's presence or absence, as the case may be, but not on both.

As in previous sections a cut-off point of 20% is selected indicating that unless at least 20% of the ratings for a symptom are ratings of presence (or absence, as the case may be) a statement on the overall reliabilty of the symptom item (referring to presence and absence) cannot be made. The symptoms sadness, joylessness, lack of energy, disruption of social functioning, slowness of thought, loss of interest, and loss of ability to concentrate were apparently present in all subjects rated as part of the intercentre exercises; and

Fig. 3. Intercentre reliability—symptoms and signs with π-values and lower and upper confidence limits (95%)

See Fig. 1 for symptom number codes.

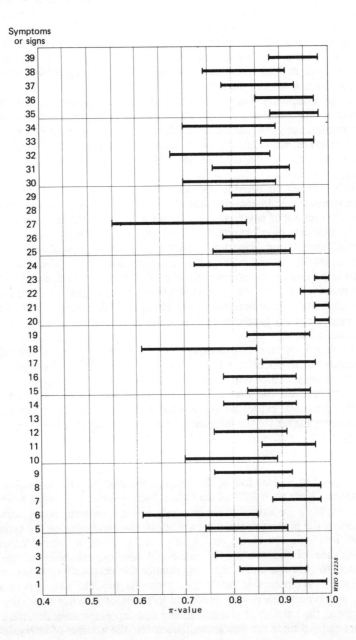

WHO 82238

hypochondriasis, ideas of impoverishment, ideas of persecution and self-reference, delusional symptoms and "other" symptoms seemed to have been absent in those patients.

A comparison of the π- and φ-values shows that the φ-value is not a very useful indicator of reliability in such situations: pairwise agreement was reached in 76% of the ratings in regard to the symptom slowness of thought, but this was agreement on presence. The corresponding φ-value is 0.06. This low value reflects insufficiency of information for a statement on the overall reliability, but it does not mean that there was poor agreement among the psychiatrists in assessing the item slowness of thought.

Seven symptoms had π-values below 0.8, but all were higher than 0.6: aggression, indecisiveness, suicidal ideas, diurnal fluctuation of mood (worse in the morning), early awakening, fitful sleep, and change of body weight. Care should be taken not to attach undue weight to the relatively low reliability of these symptoms, particularly as the reliability is still sufficiently high for subsequent analyses.

It is difficult to provide an exact interpretation of the lower rating of certain symptoms in intercentre than in intracentre exercises. In part, belonging to the same school of psychiatry may explain this; in part, the reason may lie in different amounts of information available to raters in the two situations: there was, for example, no opportunity to ask additional questions in intercentre exercises. Difficulties in language and comprehension, difficulties with technical aspects (e.g., quality of recordings), or other external difficulties related to the rating process may also lead to this phenomenon. It seems more likely that the lower reliability of a symptom, such as change of body weight, was caused by some external rating problems than by cultural differences in the interpretation of the item content.

Table A8 (Annex 1) compares the intracentre and intercentre reliability coefficients (in terms of a, π and φ) for those symptoms for which rating on both symptom presence and absence were available. The intercentre values are lower not only on the average but also individually. The variability of the reliability measures expressed as standard deviations from the arithmetic mean is three times higher for the intercentre than for the intracentre exercises. However, even the lowest π-value of 0.73 with a lower confidence limit of 0.55 ($P = 0.95$) is significantly above the critical threshold of insufficient reliability.

The reliability profile of the categories describing the patients' past history is shown in Fig. 4. For five of the items of the past history profile (see Table A9, Annex 1) less than 20% of the ratings were positive and hence a statement on the reliability for assessing the presence of the symptoms is not possible on the basis of the present sample. Nevertheless, the agreement on the symptoms' absence was high. The corresponding π-values are given in Table A9, Annex 1.

Because of the method of numerical scoring, reliability of the items referring to pronounced traits of premorbid personality, other psychopathological symptoms in adult life, continual psychic stress, precipitating stress, and type of onset was expressed in terms of π, while reliability of the items giving the number of previous manic and depressive episodes, the number of years elapsed since the first episode occurred, the number of intervals free of

Fig. 4. Reliability: intercentre (all centres combined) psychiatric history items with reliability coefficients and lower and upper confidence limits (95%)

See Fig. 2 for symptom number codes.

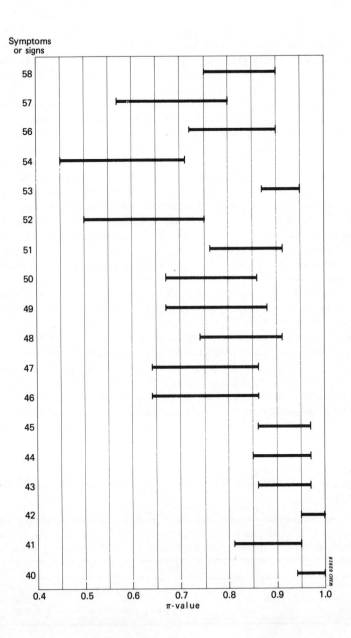

symptoms, and course and duration of present episode was computed in terms of the intraclass correlation coefficient. The correlation coefficients were transformed to vary in the range of 0.5–1.0 to obtain a scale comparable with that of the π values.

There were 12 categories for which variability of the scores was sufficient to make statements on the reliability of the rating process, both on the item's presence and on its absence. The average reliability score was 0.78 with a standard deviation of 0.09. Again this is considerably lower than in the case of the intracentre reliability exercises with a mean of 0.91. However, all the values are significantly higher than 0.5, i.e., the threshold for insufficient reliability. Five past history characteristics had confidence limits ($P = 0.95$) below 0.65: pronounced traits of premorbid personality, other psychopathological symptoms in adult life, number of previous manic episodes, number of intervals free of symptoms, and course of present episode. These items were also of comparatively low reliability in the intracentre analysis and the findings would not support the hypothesis that the past history characteristics assessed in the study are differently scored in different countries. The diagnoses according to the Basle system (regrouped into endogenous, psychogenic and other depression) could be assessed with perfect reliability ($\pi = 1.0$). With a π-value of 0.77 the reliability for a diagnostic decision according to the Teheran department was about 10% lower than in the intracentre reliability exercises. The corresponding value for the four-digit ICD diagnoses was $\pi = 0.68$.

In summary (see Table 7) the results of intercentre reliability assessments show that the level of the intercentre reliability is approximately 10% lower than that of the intracentre values. The standard deviation is considerably higher; only for the psychiatric history items is it at the same level. For some of the symptoms characteristic of patients suffering from depression, reliability statements could be made only on the assessment of those symptoms' presence, since practically no patient was without those symptoms. Other items, such as delusional symptoms, could be assessed only in terms of reliability for measuring their absence. Perfect agreement was reached in the assessment of the diagnosis in terms proposed by the Basle centre, which were regrouped into endogenous, psychogenic, and other depression. None of the items assessed was of insufficient reliability: all π-values were significantly above 0.5. Difficulties of rating recorded interviews conducted in a foreign language make it necessary to interpret those findings with caution. It is likely however that interviews in which language and other cultural barriers are not an obstacle will have even higher reliability levels—as results of intracentre exercises clearly show.

Table 7. Mean and standard deviation of π-values (and transformed intraclass correlation coefficients respectively) for the items of three sections of the rating schedule: comparison between intra- and intercentre reliability exercises

	Intracentre	Intercentre
Symptoms and signs	0.96 ($\pm$ 0.02)	0.88 ($\pm$ 0.07)
Psychiatric history	0.91 ($\pm$ 0.10)	0.83 ($\pm$ 0.11)
Diagnosis	0.92 ($\pm$ 0.09)	0.82 ($\pm$ 0.17)

4. Characteristics of the patients included in the study

Demographic and socioeconomic characteristics of the patients

As a result of the screening procedure, a total of 573 patients were selected for detailed assessment using the WHO/SADD schedule. Of these 136 were in Basle, 108 in Montreal, 108 in Nagasaki, 107 in Teheran, and 114 in Tokyo.

The distribution by age and sex[1] is shown in Table 8. The modal age group for the study population, into which 23.6% fell, was 35–44. Basle had the highest (51.4%) and Teheran the lowest (23.9%) proportion of patients aged 45 and above. Teheran had the highest percentage of patients younger than 35 years (57.9%). Male patients in the study were somewhat younger than the females: among the males 65.2% were less than 45 years, compared with 56.8% of the females in the same age category.

The distribution of the study population by sex shows a preponderance of females (58.9%), usual in studies of depression, but the within-centre proportions show certain differences. Basle and Montreal are very similar (percentage of female patients 67.7 and 66.7, respectively) and have the highest proportions of females among the patients selected for study. Tokyo was the only centre in which males (55.2%) outnumbered females (44.8%).

Most of the patients in all the centres (60.4%) were married, and only 14% were divorced, separated, or widowed. The proportion of patients who were divorced or separated was highest in Basle (15.4%) and the proportion of widowed individuals was relatively high (over 8%) in Montreal and Teheran. The

---

[1] As indicated in Chapter 1, the interpretation of sociodemographic findings was not a specific objective of this study, which did not aim to obtain representative samples. Nosocomial factors (differential tolerance of the social environment, different thresholds for help-seeking for males and females in the various cultures, etc.) have probably played an important part in the origin of differences and the data given below should serve to describe the groups studied and facilitate understanding of findings or comparisons.

highest proportion of single, never married patients was in Montreal and the lowest in Tokyo. The data on the marital status of the patients are presented in Table 9. As a whole, the study population is clearly an urban one; 89.5% of all patients live in urban or periurban areas. The proportion of patients living in rural districts encompassed by the catchment areas was 9.1% and only one centre (Nagasaki) had a sizeable proportion (25.9%) of rural patients.

The economic status of the patients described in categories "high", "medium", and "low" is shown in Table 10. Teheran was the centre with the highest proportion (55.1%) of patients in the "low economic status" category, and the two Japanese centres had the greatest numbers of patients in the "medium" category. The ratings on economic status were made in rather global terms and were probably influenced by subjective judgement. The breakdown by occupation of the patients in the different centres may be more informative (Table 11). Housewives constitute the largest single group, and their proportion is highest in Teheran. The group of unskilled and semiskilled occupations ranks second in all the centres. Skilled industrial workers constitute a surprisingly small proportion of the patients, even in centres where, as indicated in Chapter 2, a considerable part of the population is engaged in industry. If the study population is classified into gainfully employed and unemployed (including self-employed) groups, then Teheran and Basle have the highest proportions (77.6% and 69.9%) in the gainfully employed category and Nagasaki the highest proportion (44.4%) in the unemployed category.

Table 8. Percentage distribution of the patients by age and sex in the different centres

Years of age	Basle			Montreal			Nagasaki		
	M (N = 44)	F (N = 92)	All (N = 136)	M (N = 36)	F (N = 72)	All (N = 108)	M (N = 50)	F (N = 58)	All (N = 108)
Under 15	—	—	—	—	—	—	—	—	—
15–24	6.8	10.9	9.6	13.9	19.4	17.6	16.0	17.2	16.7
25–34	27.3	16.3	19.8	22.2	16.7	18.5	18.0	6.9	12.0
35–44	11.4	22.8	19.1	30.6	19.4	23.1	38.0	25.9	31.5
45–54	27.3	26.1	26.5	13.9	25.0	21.3	20.0	27.6	24.1
55–64	20.4	16.3	17.6	16.7	15.3	15.7	4.0	17.2	11.1
⩾65	6.8	7.6	7.3	2.8	4.2	3.7	4.0	5.2	4.6
Total (%)	100.0	100.0	100.0	100.0	100.0	100.0	100.0	100.0	100.0

Years of age	Teheran			Tokyo			All centres		
	M (N = 43)	F (N = 64)	All (N = 107)	M (N = 63)	F (N = 51)	All (N = 114)	M (N = 236)	F (N = 337)	All (N = 573)
Under 15	—	1.6	0.9	—	—	—	—	0.3	0.2
15–24	18.6	29.7	25.2	11.1	21.6	15.8	13.1	19.0	16.6
25–34	46.5	23.4	32.7	20.6	13.7	17.5	26.3	15.7	20.1
35–44	16.3	17.2	16.8	30.2	25.5	28.1	25.8	22.0	23.6
45–54	11.6	20.3	16.8	23.8	15.7	20.2	19.9	23.4	22.0
55–64	7.0	6.2	6.6	7.9	19.6	13.1	10.6	14.8	13.1
⩾65	—	1.6	0.9	6.3	3.9	5.3	4.2	4.7	4.5
Total (%)	100.0	100.0	100.0	100.0	100.0	100.0	100.0	100.0	100.0

Table 9. Marital status of patients (%) by centre

	Marital status					
Centre	Single never married	Married including common-law marriage	Divorced	Separated	Widowed	Total
Basle (N = 136)	26.5	53.7	11.0	4.4	4.4	100
Montreal (N = 108)	31.5	50.9	2.8	6.5	8.3	100
Nagasaki (N = 108)	21.2	65.8	5.6	0.9	6.5	100
Teheran (N = 107)	28.0	59.9	2.8	0.9	8.4	100
Tokyo (N = 114)	21.0	72.9	1.7	—	4.4	100
All centres (N = 573)	25.6	60.4	5.1	2.7	6.2	100

Table 10. Economic status of patients (%) by centre.

	Economic status				
Centre	High	Medium	Low	Impossible to estimate	Total
Basle (N = 136)	6.6	63.2	26.5	3.7	100
Montreal (N = 108)	16.7	32.4	35.2	15.7	100
Nagasaki (N = 108)	11.1	80.6	6.5	1.8	100
Teheran (N = 107)	3.7	41.2	55.1	—	100
Tokyo (N = 114)	19.3	75.4	5.3	—	100
All centres (N = 573)	11.3	59.0	25.5	4.2	100

Table 11. Distribution (%) of study population by occupation and by centre

Occupational group	Basle N = 136	Montreal N = 108	Nagasaki N = 108	Teheran N = 107	Tokyo N = 114	All centres N = 573
Professionals, executives, civil servants and freelance occupations	8.8	8.3	11.1	—	14.9	8.7
Skilled technical occupations (e.g., technicians, secretaries, nurses)	10.3	2.8	2.8	4.7	13.2	7.0
Skilled industrial workers	0.7	2.8	—	3.7	2.6	1.9
Unskilled and semiskilled workers and employees	20.6	22.1	18.5	23.4	17.6	20.4
Self-employed persons (e.g., trade, craftsmanship)	19.9	7.4	6.5	6.5	7.9	10.1
Agricultural workers	—	1.9	9.2	1.9	—	2.4
Students	2.9	3.7	5.6	4.7	4.4	4.2
Housewives	25.8	36.1	26.8	43.0	21.9	30.4
Retired persons and invalids	3.7	1.9	—	—	2.6	1.8
Unemployed	0.7	11.1	13.9	9.3	8.8	8.4
Other or not known	6.6	1.9	5.6	2.8	6.1	4.7
Total (%)	100	100	100	100	100	100

Table 12. Highest level of education reached (%) by centre

Centre	Illiterate, no school	Less than 5 years of school	5–12 years of school	More than 12 years of school, including completed or uncompleted university education	Postgraduate education completed	Unknown	Total
Basle (N = 136)	0.7	2.2	83.9	12.5	0.7	—	100
Montreal (N = 108)	0.9	3.7	67.6	23.1	2.8	1.9	100
Nagasaki (N = 108)	—	0.9	82.4	16.7	—	—	100
Teheran (N = 107)	43.0	12.2	41.1	0.9	1.9	0.9	100
Tokyo (N = 114)	—	2.6	45.6	50.0	0.9	0.9	100
All centres (N = 573)	8.4	4.2	64.9	20.6	1.2	0.7	100

The highest level of education attained by the patients in the different centres is shown in Table 12. Tokyo had a very high proportion with completed or uncompleted post-secondary school education (57 of 114, or 50%, of whom 35 are university graduates). Basle and Nagasaki had the highest proportions of patients who had completed between 5 and 12 years of school (83.8% and 82.4%). Teheran had a high proportion of illiterate patients (43%) as well as of patients who had completed fewer than 5 years of school (12.1%).

Considering all the demographic and socioeconomic characteristics of the patients included in the study, it could be concluded that the groups of patients assessed in the four centres in developed countries—Basle, Montreal, Nagasaki and Tokyo—were similar, although it is not possible to say in precisely which ways they may be different from the general population of the catchment areas. One apparent socioeconomic difference is that industrial workers (especially skilled workers) seem to be under-represented in the study population in these centres and housewives somewhat over-represented. The series of patients assessed in Teheran differs from the patients in the other centres by: (a) being, on an average, younger; (b) including a very high proportion of illiterates; (c) including a high proportion of patients of low income status.

Distribution of patients by diagnostic group

The investigators were requested to formulate a diagnosis upon completion of the assessment of every patient, and to classify their diagnosis according to two alternative classification systems, one proposed by the Basle group of investigators and the other by the Teheran centre.

The two classification schemes have certain features in common and can be regarded as complementary. The Basle system is based on nosological concepts and distinguishes between eight types of depressive condition: periodic (unipolar) depression, involutional (late) depression, circular depression (manic-depressive illness), schizoaffective depressive disorder, exhaustion depression, neurotic depression, reactive depression, and other depressive conditions. A glossary describing the clinical features of each of these types was provided to investigators. The Teheran system has five types: endogenous depression, agitated depression, mild endogenous depression, neurotic depression, and reactive depression. The first three categories can be seen as syndromes within the group of endogenous depressive illnesses. A glossary for this system was also available to investigators when they were making their diagnosis.

In every centre patients were assigned to each diagnostic group of the Basle classification (except for schizoaffective disorder in Montreal and exhaustion depression in Nagasaki), but their number varied. The reasons for this variation included differences in the age composition of the patient series (e.g., there were few diagnoses of involutional depression in centres with fewer patients in the corresponding age group) and difficulties in applying a particular diagnostic category (e.g., exhaustion depression) in all centres.

The distribution of patients according to the classification model proposed by the Basle centre is shown in Table 13. Periodic (unipolar) depression

Table 13. Distribution of patients according to the classification system proposed by the Basle centre

Centre	Periodic depression[a]			Involutional depression (late depression)			Cyclic (manic-depressive) depression			Schizo-affective disorder			Exhaustion depression			Neurotic depression			Reactive depression			Other or not classified			Total		
	% (a)	N	% (b)	% (a)	N	% (b)	% (a)	N	% (b)	% (a)	N	% (b)	% (a)	N	% (b)	% (a)	N	% (b)	% (a)	N	% (b)	% (a)	N	% (b)	% (a)	N	% (b)
Basle	10.4	20	14.7	33.3	29	21.3	28.3	13	9.6	50.0	4	2.9	67.6	25	18.4	20.3	24	17.6	27.6	16	11.8	18.5	5	3.7	23.7	136	100
Montreal	12.5	24	22.2	10.3	9	8.3	23.9	11	10.2	25.0	2	1.9	5.4	2	1.9	34.7	41	38.0	27.6	16	14.8	18.5	5	4.6	18.8	108	100
Nagasaki	27.6	53	49.1	28.7	25	23.1	23.9	11	10.2	12.5	1	0.9		—		3.4	4	3.7	12.1	7	6.5	22.2	6	5.6	18.8	108	100
Teheran	21.3	41	38.3	8.1	7	6.5	6.5	3	2.8	12.5	1	0.9	24.3	9	8.4	18.6	22	20.6	24.1	14	13.1	37.0	10	9.3	18.7	107	100
Tokyo	28.1	54	47.4	19.5	17	14.9	17.4	8	7.0		—		2.7	1	0.8	22.9	27	23.7	8.6	5	4.4	3.7	1	0.9	19.9	114	100
All centres	100	192	33.5	100	87	15.2	100	46	8.0	100	8	1.4	100	37	6.5	100	118	20.6	100	58	10.1	100	27	4.7	100	573	100

[a] % (a) = vertical percentages, i.e., by centres; % (b) = horizontal percentages, i.e., by diagnosis.

constituted the largest single group of patients in the study, with the two centres in Japan contributing over one-half of the cases. Neurotic depression was the second largest group, of whom 55% were in Basle and Montreal. The group of cases diagnosed as involutional depression was composed mainly of patients in Basle, Nagasaki, and Tokyo, with a few cases in Montreal and Teheran. The group of patients with circular (manic-depressive) depression was relatively small (8% of all cases), with Tokyo and Teheran contributing fewer cases to it than the other three centres. In the category of exhaustion depression, 91.9% of all patients were in Basle (67.6%) and Teheran (24.3%) and only three cases were so diagnosed in the remaining three centres. Depression in the context of a schizoaffective disorder was a rare condition (a total of eight cases in the study). The residual group of "other" and unclassified depressive illnesses constituted 4.7% of the study population.

The uneven distribution of the diagnostic subtypes across the centres, with very few or even no cases in some nosological categories in several of the centres, would make difficult the analysis and interpretation of results. Since the investigators agreed that the main dividing line within the continuum of different nosological varieties or syndromes of depression was that separating predominantly endogenous from predominantly psychogenic disorders, a simplified classification of the study patients was obtained by collapsing the diagnostic categories in the following way:

Periodic (unipolar) depression Involutional (late) depression Circular (manic-depressive, bipolar) depression	} *Endogenous depression*
Exhaustion depression Neurotic depression Reactive depression	} *Psychogenic depression*
Schizoaffective depressive disorder Other depressive disorder Unclassified depressive disorder	} *Other depression*

The distribution of patients according to this simplified classification is presented in Table 14. Of the total of 573 patients, 56.7% were in the endogenous group, 37.2% in the psychogenic group, and 6.1% in the "other depression" category. Endogenous depressive disorders represented a greater proportion of the total than psychogenic depressions in Nagasaki, Tokyo, Teheran, and Basle; Montreal was the only centre in which more patients were classified in the psychogenic than in the endogenous group.

Clinical characteristics of the patients in the different centres

Patient status at initial assessment

At the time of the initial assessment the majority (62.8%) of the patients in the study were being treated as inpatients. However, this preponderance of inpatients occurred almost entirely because in one centre (Basle) all the study patients, and in another (Montreal) 96.2% of the study patients were inpatients.

Table 14. Distribution of patients according to broader diagnostic groups

Centre	Endogenous[a]			Psychogenic			Other			Total	
	% (a)	N	% (b)	% (a)	N	% (b)	N	% (a)	% (b)	N	% (b)
Basle	19.1	62	45.6	30.5	65	47.8	9	25.7	6.6	136	100
Montreal	13.5	44	40.7	27.7	59	54.6	5	14.3	4.6	108	100
Nagasaki	27.4	89	82.4	5.2	11	10.2	8	22.9	7.4	108	100
Teheran	15.7	51	47.7	21.1	45	42.0	11	31.4	10.3	107	100
Tokyo	24.3	79	69.3	15.5	33	28.9	2	5.7	1.8	114	100
All centres	100	325	56.7	100	213	37.2	35	100	6.1	573	100

[a] % (a) = vertical percentages, i.e., by centre; % (b) = horizontal percentages, i.e., by diagnosis.

In Teheran, the proportions were almost equal (50.5% inpatients and 49.5% outpatients). In Tokyo and Nagasaki there were more outpatients than inpatients (69.3% outpatients in Tokyo and 67.6% in Nagasaki). Thus, while Tokyo and Nagasaki had a higher proportion of patients classified as suffering from endogenous depressions, they also had a higher proportion of outpatients than the other centres.

Sources of information used in the assessment

All patients in the study were interviewed by a psychiatrist. In addition, other sources of information were used in varying proportions of the cases to rate and record all the data covered by the WHO/SADD schedule. Interview with a relative was carried out in 65.4% of the cases in Teheran, 53.7% in Nagasaki, 37.5% in Basle, 12.3% in Tokyo, and only 5.6% in Montreal. Interviews with other informants took place in 35.3% of the cases in Basle, 31.8% in Teheran, 21.3% in Nagasaki, 17.6% in Montreal, and 1.8% in Tokyo. Observation in the ward was possible for over half of the cases in Basle and Teheran but in less than one-fifth of the cases in Montreal, Nagasaki, and Tokyo (most in Nagasaki and Tokyo were outpatients). Of all possible additional sources of information, the most frequently used was case notes from current admissions (55% of all patients assessed in the study). Case notes from previous admissions were available for 33.1% of the patients in Basle, 29.6% in Nagasaki, 15.7% in Montreal, 15% in Teheran, and for only 1 case in Tokyo.

Past history. The percentages of positive ratings on items describing the past history of the patients by diagnostic group and by centre are shown in Table 15.

Presence of an affective psychiatric disorder in a relative of the patient was reported in 28.3% of the endogenous cases and in 19.7% of the psychogenic cases. The highest proportion of patients with endogenous depression who had a family history of affective disorders was in Basle (50%), and the lowest in Teheran. Positive family history of a mental disorder of a nonaffective type was, however, slightly more frequent in the group of patients with psychogenic depressions (23.5% compared with 18.5% in the endogenous depression group). Access to informants and reliability of recall and information are factors likely to influence considerably such percentages, and therefore the data should be interpreted with caution.

The items referring to adverse early environmental influences (early separation, stressful events in childhood) were rated as present in a greater proportion of patients in the psychogenic group than in the endogenous group in all the centres. However, the considerable differences in the percentage of positive ratings (e.g., stressful events in childhood were found in 51% of the patients with psychogenic depression in Basle and in only one patient of the corresponding diagnostic group in Nagasaki) suggest that the threshold for rating varied across the centres—probably because of differing interpretations of the definition of the item, in spite of the glossary definition made available to the centres.

Table 15. Positive ratings (%) on past history items, by centre

	Endogenous depression						Psychogenic depression					
	Basle (N = 62)	Montreal (N = 44)	Nagasaki (N = 89)	Teheran (N = 51)	Tokyo (N = 79)	All centres (N = 325)	Basle (N = 65)	Montreal (N = 59)	Nagasaki (N = 11)	Teheran (N = 45)	Tokyo (N = 33)	All centres (N = 213)
History of psychiatric disorder in relatives (affective)	50.0	36.3	16.9	13.7	29.1	28.3	21.5	32.2	9.0	8.9	12.1	19.7
History of psychiatric disorder in relatives (general)	21.0	11.3	15.7	31.4	15.2	18.5	23.1	32.2	27.3	22.2	9.0	23.5
Early separation	11.3	15.9	15.7	27.4	10.1	15.4	29.2	23.7	27.3	31.1	27.3	27.7
Stressful events in childhood	33.9	29.5	4.5	13.7	10.1	16.3	51.0	35.6	9.0	40.0	18.2	37.1
Psychopathological symptoms in childhood	21.0	15.9	9.0	7.8	2.5	10.5	40.0	37.3	36.4	17.8	12.1	30.0
Psychopathological symptoms in adolescence	11.3	29.5	2.2	—	7.6	8.6	21.5	37.3	18.2	11.1	12.1	22.1
Pronounced traits of premorbid personality	27.4	45.4	—	5.9	13.9	15.7	47.7	44.1	—	20.0	42.4	37.5
General psychopathological symptoms, syndromes and disorders in adult life	14.5	15.9	3.4	3.9	6.3	8.0	36.9	39.0	27.3	6.7	12.1	26.8
Continual psychic stress	30.6	50.0	19.1	13.7	31.6	27.7	73.8	69.5	65.6	48.9	45.4	62.4
Precipitating stress	29.0	29.3	44.9	21.6	45.6	36.3	71.0	54.2	90.9	60.0	36.4	59.6

Presence of nonaffective psychiatric symptoms in the past or currently (psychopathological symptoms in childhood or adolescence and in adult life, pronounced traits of premorbid personality) was recorded more frequently in the group of patients with psychogenic depressions. Continual psychological stress and precipitating stress were rated as present in 62.4% and 59.6% of the psychogenic group and in 27.7% and 36.3% of the endogenous group. It is interesting to note that although psychological stress was more frequent in patients with psychogenic disorders, in over one-third of all the patients with endogenous depressions, precipitating stress was rated as present in connexion with the episode of inclusion.

Considering the history of affective episodes in the patients included in the study, it is worth noting that 46.3% of all patients had suffered at least one depressive episode in the past. A history of manic episodes in the past was elicited far less frequently: only 6.8% of the patients had one or more manic episodes, and only 5.4% had at least one manic and one depressive episode prior to the episode of inclusion. The highest proportion (54.4%) of patients with at least one depressive episode in the past was in Basle, and the lowest (26.2%) in Teheran. Tokyo had the highest proportions with manic episodes in the past (11.4%). The data are presented in Table 16.

Table 16. Past History—percentage patients who had previous affective episodes

Centre	At least 1 previous depressive episode	At least 1 previous manic episode	At least 1 depressive and 1 manic episode previously
Basle (N = 136)	54.4	7.3	5.1
Montreal (N = 108)	61.1	4.6	4.6
Nagasaki (N = 108)	43.5	8.3	7.4
Teheran (N = 107)	26.2	1.7	1.7
Tokyo (N = 114)	46.5	11.4	9.6
All centres (N = 573)	46.8	6.8	5.4

In summary, the ratings on past history items indicate that:

(a) The psychiatrists made the diagnosis of endogenous depressive disorders more often in patients with a history of affective illness in a relative; however, the group of patients diagnosed as psychogenic depressives more often had relatives with nonaffective psychiatric disorders.

(b) Psychiatrists made the diagnosis of psychogenic depressive illnesses more frequently in patients with adverse early environmental influence, nonaffective psychopathological symptoms in the past and in the present, pronounced traits of premorbid personality, and exposure to psychological stress.

(c) Almost half the patients had suffered at least one depressive episode before their inclusion in the study; only a small proportion had had manic episodes in the past.

Table 17. Distribution of positive ratings on symptoms by centre

	Basle	Montreal	Nagasaki	Teheran	Tokyo	All patients
Present in 76–100%	Sadness Joylessness Anxiety Tension Lack of energy [a]Disruption of social functioning Loss of interest Loss of ability to concentrate Ideas of insufficiency, etc. [a]Inability to fall asleep [a]Lack of appetite	Sadness Joylessness [a]Hopelessness Anxiety Tension Lack of energy [a]Disruption of social functioning Loss of interest Loss of ability to concentrate Ideas of insufficiency, etc.	Sadness Joylessness [a]Hopelessness Anxiety Tension Lack of energy [a]Disruption of social functioning [a]Slowness and retardation of thought [a]Indecisiveness Loss of interest Loss of ability to concentrate Ideas of insufficiency, etc. [a]Psychomotor retardation [a]Inability to fall asleep [a]Fitful, restless sleep [a]Feelings of pressure and pain	Sadness Joylessness Anxiety Lack of energy	Sadness Joylessness Anxiety Lack of energy Loss of ability to concentrate	Sadness Joylessness Anxiety Tension Lack of energy Loss of interest Loss of ability to concentrate Ideas of insufficiency, etc.
Present in 51–75%	Hopelessness Aggression, irritability Slowness and retardation of thought Indecisiveness Change of perception of time [a]Feelings of guilt and self-reproach Suicidal ideas Psychomotor retardation Lack of contact	Aggression, irritability Slowness and retardation of thought Indecisiveness Change of perception of time [a]Feelings of guilt and self-reproach Suicidal ideas Psychomotor retardation	Change of perception of time [a]Hypochondriasis Suicidal ideas Lack of contact [a]Worse in the morning Decrease of libido Early awakening Change of body weight	[a]Tension Aggression, irritability Disruption of social functioning Indecisiveness [a]Loss of interest [a]Loss of ability to concentrate Change of perception of time	Hopelessness [a]Tension Aggression, irritability Slowness and retardation of thought Indecisiveness [a]Loss of interest	Hopelessness Aggression, irritability Disruption of social functioning Slowness and retardation of thought Indecisiveness Change of perception of time Suicidal ideas

Present in 26–50%	Hypochondriasis Psychomotor agitation aChange of body weight Other somatic symptoms	aWorse in the morning Decrease of libido Early awakening Fitful, restless sleep aConstipation Feelings of pressure and pain	Psychomotor agitation Worse in the morning aEarly awakening Constipation Other somatic symptoms Other symptoms I	Lack of contact Decrease of libido Inability to fall asleep Fitful, restless sleep Lack of appetite	Feelings of guilt and self-reproach aIdeas of impoverishment aIdeas of persecution and self-reference Psychomotor agitation Other somatic symptoms	aConstipation Other symptoms

aPsychomotor agitation Lack of contact Inability to fall asleep Fitful, restless sleep Lack of appetite Change of body weight Feelings of pressure and pain aOther somatic symptoms aOther symptoms I	aHopelessness aSlowness and retardation of thought Feelings of guilt and self-reproach aIdeas of insufficiency, etc. aSuicidal ideas aIdeas of persecution and self-reference aPsychomotor retardation Worse in the evening aDecrease of libido	aIdeas of insufficiency, etc. Early awakening Inability to fall asleep Lack of appetite

aChange of perception of time Feelings of guilt and self-reproach Hypochondriasis aSuicidal ideas aPsychomotor retardation Worse in the morning aDecrease of libido aFitful, restless sleep aChange of body weight aFeelings of pressure and pain	Psychomotor retardation Lack of contact Decrease of libido Early awakening Inability to fall asleep Fitful, restless sleep Lack of appetite Change of body weight Feelings of pressure and pain	Feelings of guilt and self-reproach Hypochondriasis Psychomotor agitation Worse in the morning Constipation Other somatic symptoms Other symptoms I

Continued on page 56

Table 17. (cont.)

	Basle	Montreal	Nagasaki	Teheran	Tokyo	All patients
Present in 1–25%	Ideas of persecution and self-reference Delusions of guilt Hypochondriacal delusions Delusions of impoverishment Other delusions Worse in the evening [a]Other symptoms I Other symptoms II	[a]Hypochondriasis Ideas of impoverishment Ideas of persecution and self-reference Delusions of guilt Hypochondriacal delusions Delusions of impoverishment Other delusions Worse in the evening Other symptoms II	Delusions of guilt Hypochondriacal delusions Delusions of impoverishment Other delusions Worse in the evening Other symptoms II	[a]Hypochondriasis Ideas of impoverishment Other delusions Other symptoms II	Ideas of impoverishment Ideas of persecution and self-reference Delusions of guilt Hypochondriacal delusions Other delusions [a]Lack of contact Worse in the evening [a]Other symptoms I Other symptoms II	Ideas of impoverishment Ideas of persecution and self-reference Delusions of guilt Hypochondriacal delusions Worse in the evening Delusions of impoverishment Other delusions Other symptoms II
Absent	Change of perception of time	Change of body weight	Aggression, irritability	Delusions of guilt Hypochondriacal delusions Delusions of impoverishment	Delusions of impoverishment	—

[a] Indicates symptoms for which the frequency (by quartile) of positive ratings in a centre deviated from the average for all patients.

Symptoms of current episode ("last week" and "symptoms anytime in current episode" combined)

The frequency of positive ratings on symptoms is presented in Table 17. To simplify the presentation of these results, symptom ratings of 1 (mild) and 2 (severe) have been collapsed into "presence of symptom", and the frequencies obtained in the different centres combined into four quartiles: presence of the symptom in 76–100% of all the patients assessed, presence in 51–75%, presence in 26–50%, and presence in 1–25%. Symptoms that were never rated as present are listed on the bottom line of the table. Symptoms that appeared in a particular quartile in one of the centres but did not appear in the same quartile of the distribution for all patients in the study are marked by an asterisk.

The table leads to several conclusions:

(1) The most frequent symptoms in all the centres combined were sadness, joylessness, anxiety, tension, lack of energy, loss of interest, loss of ability to concentrate, and ideas of insufficienty, inadequacy, and worthlessness. This set of "core" characteristics of depression (present in 76% of the cases) was considerably augmented in Nagasaki (where it included 9 further symptoms), less so in Basle and Montreal, and somewhat reduced in Tokyo and Teheran. It is of interest that anxiety and tension appear to be among the most frequent symptoms of depressive disorders in all the centres. Ideas of insufficiency, one of the most frequent symptoms in Basle, Montreal and Nagasaki, is less frequently rated as present in Tokyo and still less frequently in Teheran.

(2) Suicidal ideas were present in 59% of the patients (all centres combined) but were less frequent in Teheran and Tokyo (in 46% and 41% respectively).

(3) Delusions of any kind appeared to be rare among the study population in all centres; they occurred in 2–5% of all patients. In one of the centres (Teheran) no depressive delusions were rated as present, and in another centre (Tokyo) one type of delusion (impoverishment) did not occur at all.

(4) Hypochondriasis (not amounting to hypochondriacal delusions) was less frequent (34% of all patients) than might be expected. It was least frequent in Montreal (22%) and Teheran (17%).

(5) Feelings of guilt and self-reproach (which have been claimed not to occur in depressive patients in all cultures) occurred in varying proportions of the patients in all centres, but were more prevalent in Basle and Montreal (68% in Basle, 58% in Montreal, 41% in Nagasaki, 32% in Teheran, and 48% in Tokyo).

(6) Somatic symptoms (other than feelings of pressure and pain, constipation, lack of appetite, change of body weight, and loss of libido) were rated as present in a considerable proportion (40%) of all patients. They were less frequent in Basle (32%) and Montreal (27%) and more frequent in Teheran (57%).

(7) Psychomotor agitation had an average frequency of 42% (all patients combined). Teheran was the only centre in which it occurred with a markedly higher frequency (64%).

(8) Altogether 40% of the patients exhibited during the assessment "other" symptoms, i.e., symptoms for which no precoded items were provided in the schedule. For most of these patients narrative descriptions of the "other" symptoms were written by the investigators.

In practically all centres several categories of "other" symptoms emerge from these descriptions: (a) various somatic symptoms and complaints (e.g., low-back pain, nausea, headaches, acrocyanosis, sweating, tremor, dysmenorrhoea or amenorrhea); (b) obsessional symptoms (e.g., repetitive thoughts, checking); (c) phobias and panic attacks; (d) sexual dysfunction (impotence, frigidity); (e) feeling of fatigue; (f) hysterical motor or sensory disorder; (g) possible side-effects of drugs (e.g., dry mouth, vertigo). More "exotic" symptoms and complaints were exceedingly rare (e.g., a single case of a "possession experience" in Nagasaki, or complaints of spermatorrhoea in one patient in Teheran).

A comparison of the groups of patients diagnosed as having endogenous and psychogenic depressive disorders in the different centres showed that psychiatrists clearly made their diagnoses using information other than symptoms: the sets of 15 most frequently positive items in the two groups were very similar in all centres (Table 18). Therefore, in Table 19 only those symptoms are presented for which greatest differences emerged in the percentages of cases where they were rated as present in the two diagnostic groups. The sets of five symptoms in each centre that were responsible for the greatest percentage differences between endogenous and psychogenic depressive disorders did indeed include symptoms that are generally considered diagnostically important (e.g., worse in the morning, worse in the evening, early awakening, slowness or retardation of thought, psychomotor retardation). These sets of symptoms, however, were not the only or the best differentiating characteristics of the endogenous and psychogenic depressive disorders. As will be demonstrated in Chapter 5, the symptoms that psychiatrists in the centres used to discriminate between the two major subtypes of depression could only be identified through a multivariate statistical analysis.

Onset, course, and treatment of the episode of inclusion

In most of the patients included in the study (69.3%) the onset of the depressive illness was rated as slow or insidious. The proportions of patients with insidious and with sudden acute onset differed little across the centres.

The course of the disorder up to the time of the interview was rated as steadily deteriorating or fluctuating in 57.2%, as stable (with or without some improvement after an initial deterioration) in 21.6%, and as steadily improving in 17.6%.

Only 16.7% had not received any treatment by the time of the initial assessment, and 79.5% were on drug treatment, which was combined with some form of psychotherapy in 20.2%. Only 12 patients of the total of 573 were receiving electroconvulsive treatment, with or without drug treatment. Psychotherapy (individual or group) was the exclusive form of treatment in only 9 patients.

Table 18. The 15 most frequently positive symptoms (all centres)

Rank	Endogenous depression			Psychogenic depression		
	Male	Female	Total	Male	Female	Total
1.	Lack of energy	Sadness	Sadness	Sadness	Sadness	Sadness
2.	Sadness	Joylessness	Lack of energy	Joylessness	Joylessness	Joylessness
3.	Joylessness	Lack of energy	Joylessness	Anxiety	Anxiety	Anxiety
4.	Anxiety	Anxiety	Anxiety	Lack of energy	Lack of energy	Lack of energy
5.	Loss of interest	Loss of interest	Loss of interest	Loss of interest	Tension	Tension
6.	Loss of ability to concentrate	Lack of appetite	Loss of ability to concentrate	Ideas of insufficiency, etc.	Aggression, irritability	Aggression, irritability
7.	Tension	Loss of ability to concentrate	Tension	Tension	Inability to fall asleep	Loss of interest
8.	Ideas of insufficiency, etc.	Tension	Disruption of social functioning	Disruption of social functioning	Lack of appetite	Ideas of insufficiency, etc.
9.	Disruption of social functioning	Disruption of social functioning	Ideas of insufficiency, etc.	Hopelessness	Suicidal ideas	Hopelessness
10.	Slowness and retardation of thought	Ideas of insufficiency, etc.	Lack of appetite	Loss of ability to concentrate	Loss of interest	Suicidal ideas
11.	Hopelessness	Hopelessness	Hopelessness	Aggression, irritability	Ideas of insufficiency, etc.	Inability to fall asleep
12.	Indecisiveness	Fitful, restless sleep	Indecisiveness	Indecisiveness	Hopelessness	Lack of appetite
13.	Decrease of libido	Indecisiveness	Slowness and retardation of thought	Suicidal ideas	Loss of ability to concentrate	Disruption of social functioning
14.	Psychomotor retardation	Inability to fall asleep	Inability to fall asleep	Inability to fall asleep	Disruption of social functioning	Loss of ability to concentrate
15.	Inability to fall asleep	Early awakening	Fitful, restless sleep	Lack of appetite	Fitful, restless sleep	Fitful, restless sleep

Table 19. Symptoms rated as present with greatest percentage difference between the groups of endogenous and psychogenic depressive disorders by centre

% difference = (% positive ratings in endogenous group) − (% positive ratings in psychogenic group)

Basle		Montreal		Nagasaki		Teheran		Tokyo		All patients	
Worse in the evening	−55	Psychomotor retardation	33	Early awakening	49	Early awakening	41	Suicidal ideas	−38	Early awakening	33
Worse in the morning	46	Constipation	30	Worse in the morning	44	Lack of contact	29	Aggression, irritability	−34	Worse in the morning	32
Early awakening	38	Slowness or retardation of thought	28	Aggression, irritability	−35	Loss of interest	28	Lack of contact	27	Slowness or retardation of thought	26
Slowness or retardation of thought	28	Suicidal ideas	−26	Ideas of impoverishment	31	Loss of ability to concentrate	27	Sadness	26	Psychomotor retardation	23
Aggression, irritability	25	Aggression, irritability	−23	Disruption of social functioning	29	Worse in the evening	−26	Loss of ability to concentrate	26	Suicidal ideas	22
Decrease of libido	−23									Aggression, irritability	−22

Summary and conclusions

Following the initial screening of consecutive admissions or outpatient attendances, a total of 573 patients with functional depressive disorders were selected for an evaluation with the WHO Schedule for Standardized Assessment of Depressive Disorders (WHO/SADD). Patients in all age groups above 15 were included in this series. The series examined had more female patients in all centres but one. The mean age of the males was lower than that of the females.

The vast majority of the patients were urban residents, except in Nagasaki where a sizeable proportion of rural residents was included. Most of the patients were classified into the medium economic status category and—with the exception of Teheran where a substantial minority were illiterate—had attained a reasonably good level of education. The biggest single occupational group was that of housewives.

The diagnoses made in the centres on every patient were classified according to two alternative classification systems, one proposed by the Basle and the other by the Teheran centre. Since, however, the numbers of patients in each of the types of such detailed classifications were too small to permit analysis and comparisons, the categories were collapsed into a simplified tripartite scheme encompassing *endogenous* depressive disorders (56.7%), *psychogenic* depressions (37.2%), and *other* depressive conditions (6.1%). In all centres but one, endogenous cases constituted the largest category.

Psychiatrists seem to have made diagnoses of the two major groups of patients with endogenous and psychogenic depressive disorders on the basis of differences in their past history. More patients diagnosed as endogenous depressives than those called psychogenic depressives had a family history of an affective disorder: more patients considered to have psychogenic illnesses had a family history of a nonaffective mental disorder. The diagnosis of a psychogenic depressive group was made more frequently in patients who were rated positive on items: adverse environmental influences (e.g., early separation, continual or precipitating stress), abnormal premorbid personality traits, and past or present nonaffective psychopathological symptoms. Almost every second patient in the study had had at least one depressive episode in the past. Only a small proportion, however, had suffered manic episodes.

With regard to the symptomatology of the inclusion episode, in all centres the patients exhibited a fairly uniform "core" of depressive symptoms (sadness, joylessness, anxiety, tension, lack of energy, loss of interest, loss of ability to concentrate, and ideas of insufficiency) which was similar in the two major diagnostic groups. The frequency of individual symptoms varied to a certain extent in the different centres but, with a few exceptions, no marked differences in the phenomenology of depressive states were observed. The additional (or "other") symptoms that were recorded in an open-ended way, where they occurred, fell into several categories and were of a nature often described in depressive illnesses. There were remarkably few, if any, "culture-specific" symptoms that occurred in one centre but not in others.

Diagnoses of endogenous and psychogenic depressions were apparently made on information other than symptoms: no fixed pattern of symptoms allowing a clear-cut demarcation of the two types of condition could be elicited with the univariate mode of analysis.

In most of the patients, the onset of the condition was slow and insidious rather than sudden or acute. At the time of initial assessment, the great majority of the patients were receiving drug treatment, and only a few were receiving either electroconvulsive therapy or only psychotherapy.

5. *Characteristics of depressive disorders: discrimination between endogenous and psychogenic depression*

Introduction

It should be stressed that the fact that certain symptoms are found in patients labelled as suffering from "endogenous" or "psychogenic" depression does not confirm the existence of such groups of conditions as an entity or disease: all that consistent association between a symptom pattern and a diagnosis means is that the psychiatrists who made the diagnoses used a diagnostic convention and a glossary consistently and well. In this sense this chapter is examining the capacity of psychiatrists to use a given diagnostic system; to learn a new system (or systems) and use it well. This remains true whether it be symptoms, factor scores, or any other derivation from the material collected in this study.

The second purpose of these analyses is to contribute to the evidence about the usefulness of some of the multivariate analyses in the examination of clinical research questions.

The univariate approach to the statistical analysis of data describing depressive disorders, presented in the foregoing chapter, revealed a number of differences between the patients assessed in the five field research centres. It also indicated that the frequency distributions of individual symptoms characteristic of groups of patients assigned by the investigators to different classification rubrics for depressive disorders followed a predictable pattern. However, the univariate approach examines single attributes of the disorder in isolation from one another and ignores the correlations that could be expected to exist among the variables. Therefore, the univariate analysis does not permit definitive conclusions about the extent to which the clinical pictures presented by those patients who were classified into each of the two major diagnostic groups of endogenous and psychogenic depression were different, or about the overall magnitude and direction of the differences—all variables considered— between patients in the several centres.

An analysis that would at the same time take into consideration all or most of the variables assessed with the rating schedule should be multivariate. However, even the relatively limited number of variables that can be derived from the Schedule for Standardized Assessment of Depressive Disorders (WHO/SADD) may prove difficult to handle and present an obstacle when it comes to disentangling and interpreting complex relations between characteristics of the patients. This problem was resolved by reducing the number of variables by condensing and transforming the correlated variables into uncorrelated ones, to simplify further analyses.

The statistical technique that was adopted for such data reduction was factor analysis. Recent and earlier controversies about the usefulness of factors (e.g., in the analysis of psychopathology) do not apply here: factors are not used to *make* the diagnosis but to *describe* the material in a manner allowing the identification of patterns that otherwise remain hidden.

Characteristics of the technique of factor analysis

A factor is an abstract, mathematically derived variable that explains the correlations observed among a large number of empirically assessed variables. The variance that occurs in multiple measurements obtained in behavioural research can be reduced to a variance on a limited number of factors.

There are two different approaches to the use of the factor concept in data reduction. The first assumes that a specified number of hypothetical factors underlie the data matrix, tests this *a priori* factor model for its fit of the data, and modifies it as necessary until a fit is obtained. In the second approach the original set of variables is examined to discover its structure without making any prior assumptions about specific underlying factors. The second approach (which was used in the analyses reported below) involves the following steps.

If for each patient two characteristics, x_1 and x_2, are measured, then each individual may be represented as a point in an x_1, x_2 coordinate system. The "clouds" of points corresponding to each patient's position with regard to these variables may turn out to be distributed as shown in Fig. 5. In such a situation the patients' positions can be described in a different coordinate system, with the property that the new first axis goes in the direction of greatest variance while the second is orthogonal to it.

In this sense, changing a coordinate system simply means replacing the original variables by a suitable linear combination of them. The new axes, corresponding to factors or principal components, should be orthogonal to each other (i.e., uncorrelated) and the first factor should explain as much of the variance as any linear combination of the original items could, etc.

Fig. 5. Choice of an optimal coordinate system to describe the data

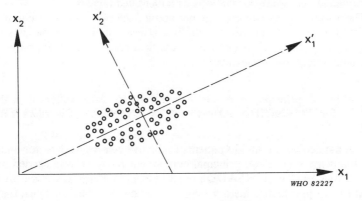

The two approaches mentioned above of replacing the original items by a set of linear combinations of the original items are usually referred to as factor analysis. The first approach requires some assumptions concerning the structure underlying the data; the second requires none. Since specific assumptions of this kind may be difficult to make, especially in a cross-cultural study, principal component analysis was performed to reduce the number of items to a set of factors that could be more easily handled. The exact configuration of the principal component structure is not unique. One factor solution can be transformed (i.e., rotated) into another without violating the basic assumptions or the mathematical properties of the solution. There are various ways of rotating the structure obtained in an initial factor analysis. The method that was considered most appropriate for the data obtained in the study was an orthogonal rotation of the new coordinate system—i.e., a rotation of the principal components to "simplify" the columns of the loading matrix. This procedure facilitates the interpretation of the factors in terms of the original items.

Usually, a linear transformation and a rotation of a coordinate system do not reduce the number of axes. However, the principal components are ordered according to how much of the variation of the data they explain. Factors[1] with small variances can be eliminated and only those with large variances are retained for further analysis. The factors can be expressed as linear combinations of the original variables, or the original variables can be expressed as linear combinations of the new factors. In this study, the coefficients that formed the linear combination of the factors that describe an original variable (i.e., the factor loadings) were ignored if their absolute values were less than or equal to 0.4[2] (i.e., original items with a factor loading greater than 0.4 were considered important). This must be an arbitrary decision, as there is no direct mathematical justification for selecting a cut-off level for

---

[1] The words "factor" and "principal component" are used synonymously.
[2] The range of the factor loading is −1 to +1.

factor loadings. A cut-off at 0.4 seems to be sufficiently high to omit items that may have only weak correlations with identified factors.

The 15 factors, explaining together about 50% of the total variation, were considered to be sufficient for a quantitative description of the patients in the study; this allowed comparisons across the field research centres and between the different diagnostic subgroups.

Application of principal component analysis to data collected with the Schedule for Standardized Assessment of Depressive Disorders (WHO/SADD)

The data collected on 573 patients in the five centres were factor-analysed in the following way. First, principal component analysis[1] was carried out on items 1.9 to 1.16 (Part 1 of SADD), the 39 symptom items in section 2A (Part 2), and the 19 psychiatric history items in section 2B (Part 2). Thus, the total number of variables used as input was 66. The items belonging to different parts of the instrument (sociodemographic background, symptoms of current episode and psychiatric history) were handled as a single data set to obtain factors that cut across the different categories of information, in the expectation that such factors might provide clues to a more parsimonious description of the phenomenology of depressive disorders in a cross-cultural context. Once a series of factors, or principal components, was obtained, the factor loadings were examined and a tentative clinical interpretation of their content was formulated. The distribution of factor scores was tabulated according to field research centres and by major diagnostic subtype of depression.

As a second step in the analysis, the factor scores were subjected to a two-way multivariate analysis of variance to test for differences in the overall factor profiles of depressive patients among the centres and between diagnostic groups. Factor scores were also used in a discriminant function analysis (see penultimate section in this chapter) to determine the accuracy of possible discrimination and identify the variables that may have been decisive for the psychiatric diagnosis of endogenous and psychogenic depression.

Factors describing the total study population (all centres combined)

The first 15 factors (principal components) explained approximately 50% of the variance in the SADD data, and it was decided to limit the interpretation of the results of this analysis to them (Factor 16—Diurnal fluctuations in mood—is described below, but not used in further analyses). Other factors—i.e., components that emerged after the first 15—made marginal and diminishing contributions to the explanation of the variance in the data and were discounted because of their low stability (see the next section).

The naming of factors is a somewhat arbitrary procedure, which should be guided by common sense. In naming the 15 principal components listed

---

[1] The numbers of items mentioned here refer to the 4th draft of the WHO/SADD schedule.

below, the aim was to choose labels providing "shorthand" descriptions of the content of the factors that would at the same time correspond to clinical terms.

Table 20 summarizes the 15 principal components and indicates the variance explained by them jointly and individually.

Table 20. Fifteen factors (principal components) explaining approximately 50% of the variance on SADD data, all field research centres combined (573 patients)

Factor	% Variance explained	Cumulative % variance explained
1. Anergia/retardation	10.1	10.1
2. Previous manic episodes	5.2	15.3
3. Abnormal personality	4.2	19.5
4. Previous depressive episodes (unspecified number)	3.4	22.9
5. Depressive delusions	3.2	26.1
6. Dejection	3.0	29.1
7. Marital status	2.7	31.8
8. Socioeconomic status	2.7	34.5
9. Sleep disturbance	2.5	37.0
10. Anxiety/agitation	2.2	39.2
11. Previous manic episodes (unspecified number)	2.2	41.4
12. Hypochondriasis	2.1	43.5
13. Other symptoms	1.9	45.4
14. Changed appetite and body weight	1.9	47.3
15. Employment: working hours	1.8	49.1

A more detailed description and discussion of each factor follows:

Factor 1 (*Anergia/retardation*). This factor, which out of the set of 15 explains the highest proportion of the variance, has the following item loadings:

Item	Loading
Loss of interest	0.668
Psychomotor retardation	0.656
Slowness of thought	0.650
Indecisiveness	0.620
Lack of energy	0.609
Loss of ability to concentrate	0.603
Lack of contact	0.572
Joylessness	0.488
Changed perception of time	0.481
Disruption of social functioning	0.475
Decrease of libido	0.459
Sadness	0.415

The highest loadings are on items describing a syndrome of anergic retarded depression, with which less specific items of depressive symptomatology, such as joylessness, sadness and decrease of libido, correlate, as could be clinically predicted. The emergence of this principal component as the first factor in the analysis suggests that the syndrome of anergic retarded depression was manifested in a similar and consistent manner in all centres.

Factor 2 (*Previous manic episodes*). The loadings of this factor are as follows:

Item	Loading
Number of previous manic episodes	0.934
Number of symptom-free intervals	0.882
Number of years since the first manic episode	0.836

The appearance of these three items as a single factor indicates only that the investigators rated consistently: the greater the number of manic episodes in the past, the greater also the number of intervals and the number of years elapsed since the first one.

Factor 3 (*Abnormal personality*). As will be demonstrated below, this factor is of some significance in discriminating between diagnostic subgroups of depressive patients. It is loaded by:

Item	Loading
Other psychopathological symptoms, syndromes, and disorders in adult life	0.699
Psychopathological symptoms in adolescence	0.684
Pronounced traits of premorbid personality	0.683
Psychopathological symptoms in childhood	0.513

Two other items that also load this factor but failed to reach the 0.4 level of inclusion are "stressful events in childhood" and "continual psychic stress".

The item "other psychopathological symptoms, syndromes and disorders in adult life" covers the presence of symptomatology other than affective (e.g., non-affective psychotic or neurotic illnesses, psychosomatic disorders, drug or alcohol abuse) in adult life prior to the affective episode of inclusion. The item of psychopathological symptoms in adolescence excludes disturbances that were clearly affective. The item of psychopathological symptoms in childhood includes a variety of problems—such as speech, sleep, and sphincter control disturbances, tics, conduct disorders, and any other condition that had necessitated treatment or consultations by a psychiatrist. Pronounced traits of premorbid personality were defined in the glossary as "striking behaviour or suffering from psychic experiences that are not caused by the present attack or by other psychiatric illness but by the structure of the personality". The items loading this factor are therefore somewhat heterogeneous and cover both abnormal personality traits and past history of psychiatric disorder other than affective. Hence, the label "abnormal personality" for this factor should be regarded with some caution, bearing in mind that it covers a wider spectrum of disturbances.

Factor 4 (*Previous depressive episodes, unspecified number*). This factor is loaded by three items:

Item	Loading
Number of previous depressive episodes unknown	0.841
Number of years since first depressive episode unknown	0.783
Number of symptom-free intervals unknown	0.780

The factor simply indicates that depressive episodes had occurred in a proportion of the patients in the past but their number could not be determined from the information available.

Factor 5 (*Depressive delusions*). The item loadings are as follows:

Item	Loading
Delusions of impoverishment	0.774
Delusions of guilt	0.749
Hypochondriacal delusions	0.480
Ideas of impoverishment	0.464
Ideas of persecution and reference	0.420

All the items refer either to the present state (last week) or to any other time during the inclusion episode. With the exception of the ideas of persecution or reference, they are of a "clearly" depressive nature. The fact that they load a single factor indicates that delusions (or ideas) of different content— impoverishment, guilt, hypochondriasis, persecution and reference—tend to be intercorrelated.

Factor 6 (*Dejection*). This factor is loaded by:

Item	Loading
Hopelessness	0.641
Feelings of guilt and self-reproach	0.518
Ideas of insufficiency, inadequacy and worthlessness, lack of self-confidence	0.414
Sadness	0.406

The items are indications of a depressive "posture" or outlook and refer to the changed attitudes to self, others, and the future arising out of a depressive mood. Therefore, the label "dejection" was chosen for this factor.

Factor 7 (*Marital status*). This factor is loaded by two items:

Item	Loading
Single	−0.909
Married	+0.831

The item content simply indicates that the marital status of the patients was recorded with relatively few errors.

Factor 8 (*Socioeconomic status*). The loadings are:

Item	Loading
Middle socioeconomic status	+0.869
Low socioeconomic status	−0.875

The inverse correlation of the two items in Factor 8 indicates that the socioeconomic status was recorded consistently by the investigators.

Factor 9 (*Sleep disturbance*). This factor is loaded by the following items:

Item	Loading
Fitful, restless sleep	0.763
Inability to fall asleep	0.721

The item "early awakening" also appeared on this factor but its loading was 0.379—i.e., it fell short of the 0.4 cut-off level selected.

Factor 10 (*Anxiety/agitation*). This factor is loaded by:

Item	Loading
Anxiety	0.675
Psychomotor agitation	0.629
Tension	0.628

The content of this factor is self-explanatory.

Factor 11 (*Previous manic episodes—unspecified number*). The loadings are

Item	Loading
Number of previous manic episodes unknown	0.907
Number of years since first manic episode unknown	0.907

This factor is similar to Factor 4, which refers to unspecified number of depressive episodes.

Factor 12 (*Hypochondriasis*). This factor is loaded by:

Item	Loading
Feelings of pressure and pain	0.639
Hypochondriasis	0.601

The appearance of these two items on one factor indicates that excessive concern with bodily functions and health is often accompanied by actual complaints of pressure and pain in different parts of the body.

Factor 13 (*Other symptoms*). The loadings of this factor are:

Item	Loading
Other symptoms (item 39, Fig. 1)	0.772
Other symptoms (item 38, Fig. 1)	0.668

The two open-ended items were provided for recording psychiatric symptoms not covered elsewhere in this schedule. The two "other symptoms" items are correlated in this factor, but because of their open-ended nature, it is not possible to give the factor a clinical interpretation.

Factor 14 (*Changed appetite and body weight*). The loadings are:

Item	Loading
Lack of appetite	0.689
Change of body weight	0.649

The factor content is self-explanatory.

Factor 15 (*Employment: working hours*). The factor is loaded by:

Item	Loading
Hours of work: 10–34 per week	0.853
Hours of work: 35 or more per week	−0.769

The inverse correlation of the items with the factor indicates simply that this information was recorded consistently.

Factor 16 (*Diurnal fluctuations of mood*). The loadings of this factor are:

Item	Loading
Worse in the morning	0.735
Worse in the evening	−0.735

The factor is self-explanatory.

Stability of the factors and limits on their interpretation

Factor analysis can be used for many different purposes in behavioural and psychopathological research: to test or generate hypotheses about dimensions underlying observable manifestations of behaviour, to identify hypothetical entities (source traits) causally connected with specific test performance (surface traits), or to reduce large data sets to more manageable amounts of information. As has been pointed out, the explicit purpose for which principal component analysis was used in the present study was data reduction, necessary to facilitate comparisons of groups of patients in the different centres or in different diagnostic categories. As indicated in the foregoing section, the 66 original variables on which information had been collected with SADD were reduced to 15 principal components that explained 50% of the variance in the data. This implies that some descriptive information was lost in the process. The lost information is contained in the ratings on a large number of items, each of them explaining independently a small fraction of the variance. Some of these items might be of little relevance to the description of depressive states while others could be important. For example, the item "history of psychiatric disorder in relatives" did not load any of the first 16 factors, although its importance is obvious. Therefore, it is not possible to make generalizations about the importance of individual items on the basis of factor analysis alone. As will be demonstrated in subsequent sections of this chapter, only the combination of factor analysis with other methods of analysis can provide the answers to specific questions about the importance of individual variables and groups of variables.

Before employing the factors as input to other statistical analyses, it was necessary to examine the problem of their stability and replicability in relation to sample size. Since no independent series of patients was available for a replication, principal components analysis was carried out on a systematic subsample of the original study population, which was obtained by selecting every second patient from the group of all patients. The results are shown in Table 21. It is evident that most of the first 16 factors obtained from the analysis of the study population as a whole could be replicated in almost identical form on this subsample. The cut-off point (0.4) for the listing of factor loadings was identical in the two analyses.

There are, however, several differences between the two series of factors. Firstly, Factor 6 (dejection) obtained from the total patient group had no counterpart among the factors derived in the replication analysis and seemed to have been absorbed in Factor 1. Secondly, Factor 5 (depressive delusions)

Table 21. Stability (replicability) of the 16 factors

Factor analysis based on data on all patients			Items	Factor analysis based on a random sample (every 2nd) from the group of all patients		
% Variance explained	Order of appearance of factor	Loadings		Loadings	Order of appearance of factor	% Variance explained
10.1	1	0.668	Loss of interest	0.739	1	11.2
		0.656	Psychomotor retardation	0.614		
		0.650	Slowness of thought	0.663		
		0.620	Indecisiveness	0.636		
		0.609	Lack of energy	0.608		
		0.603	Lack of ability to concentrate	0.597		
		0.572	Lack of contact	0.489		
		0.488	Joylessness	0.752		
		0.481	Changed perception of time	0.529		
		0.475	Disruption of social functioning	0.494		
		0.459	Decrease of libido	0.399		
		0.415	Sadness	0.669		
			Hopelessness	0.622		
			Ideas of insufficiency	0.575		
			Severity of depression	0.496		
			Suicidal ideas	0.439		
5.2	2	0.934	No. of previous manic episodes	0.954	3	4.5
		0.882	No. of symptom-free intervals	0.925		
		0.836	No. of years since first manic episode	0.875		
4.2	3	0.699	Other psychopathological symptoms in adult life	0.675	2	5.2
		0.684	Psychopathological symptoms in adolescence	0.770		
		0.683	Pronounced traits of premorbid personality	0.594		
		0.513	Psychopathological symptoms in childhood	0.583		
			Stressful events in childhood	0.497		
3.4	4	0.841	No. of previous depressive episodes unknown	0.843	4	4.1
		0.783	No. of years since first depressive episode unknown	0.786		
		0.780	No. of symptom-free intervals unknown	0.714		

3.2	5	0.774	Delusions of impoverishment	—	11	2.3
		0.749	Delusions of guilt	0.530		
		0.480	Hypochondriacal delusions	—		
		0.464	Ideas of impoverishment	0.498		
		0.420	Ideas of persecution and reference	0.628		
			Other delusions	0.570		
—	—		Hypochondriacal delusions	0.776	12	2.2
			Delusions of impoverishment	0.708		
3.0	6	0.641	Hopelessness	—	—	—
		0.518	Feelings of guilt and self-reproach	-0.898	5	3.3
		0.414	Ideas of insufficiency, etc.	0.841		
		0.406	Sadness	0.567		
2.7	7	-0.909	Single	0.817	6	3.3
		0.831	Married	-0.868		
		0.577	Age	0.405		
2.7	8	0.869	Middle economic status			
		-0.875	Low economic status			
			Education			
2.5	9	0.763	Fitful, restless sleep	0.684	10	2.4
		0.721	Inability to fall asleep	0.720		
2.2	10	0.675	Anxiety	0.668	9	2.6
		0.629	Psychomotor agitation	0.551		
		0.628	Tension	0.658		
2.2	11	0.907	No. of previous manic episodes unknown	0.876	8	2.8
		0.907	No. of years since first manic episode unknown	0.904		
2.1	12	0.639	Feelings of pressure and pain	—	—	—
		0.601	Hypochondriasis	—	—	—

Continued on page 74

Table 21 (cont.)

	Factor analysis based on data on all patients			Factor analysis based on a random sample (every 2nd) from the group of all patients	
% Variance explained	Order of appearance of factor	Loadings	Items	Loadings	Order of appearance of factor	% Variance explained
1.9	13	0.772 0.668	Other symptoms (item 39, Fig. 1) Other symptoms (item 38, Fig. 1)	0.650 0.713	14	1.9
1.9	14	0.689 0.649	Lack of appetite Change of body weight	0.647 0.737	15	1.9
1.8	15	0.853 −0.769	Hours of work: 10–34 Hours of work: 35 or more		— —	— —
	16	0.735 −0.735	Worse in the morning Worse in the evening Precipitating stress	−0.673 0.632 0.566	7	2.9
—	—		Duration of episode Type of work	0.768 0.575	13	2.1

obtained from the analysis of the total series was split into two separate factors (11 and 12) in the replication analysis. Thirdly, Factor 12 (hypochondriasis) did not appear at all among the first 16 factors in the replication analysis. Fourthly, a new factor (13), related to the duration and type of onset of the episode, emerged among the first 16 factors in the replication analysis without having an identifiable counterpart in the total series analysis.

On the whole it could be concluded that, with the exception of Factors 6 (dejection) and 12 (hypochondriasis), the factors obtained in the analysis of the total series of patients were stable and internally replicable.

Differences between the groups of depressive patients assessed in the five centres: results of multivariate analysis of variance based on factor scores

Differences between the centres in terms of the frequency distributions of individual variables describing the patients have been outlined in Chapter 4. Univariate analysis examines individual variables separately and cannot estimate the real magnitude and importance of such differences since some or many may be due to latent interactions between variables. For example, one centre may have a relative excess of patients exhibiting syndromes of endogenous depression, and at the same time the age distribution of the patients in that centre may be skewed towards the older age groups. In such a case the age distribution of the patients might explain the predominance of endogenous illnesses, and this hypothesis could be tested statistically by controlling one of the variables involved. With many variables interacting with each other, however, univariate significance tests become extremely complicated; furthermore, they cannot tell how significant the differences between patient groups would be if all the variables describing them were considered together. Answers to such questions can only be provided by multivariate statistical approaches.

To test for overall differences in the characteristics of depressive patients between the centres, factor profiles were constructed for the patients in each centre out of the averaged factor scores[1] on the first principal components (see Table 22). As a subsequent step, a two-way multivariate analysis of variance (MANOVA) was carried out on the factor profiles.

The following two null hypotheses were tested:

Hypothesis 1. If any differences exist between the centres in terms of the 15-variate factor profiles, then such differences would be of the same magnitude and direction in the two major diagnostic groups of endogenous and psychogenic depressive disorders. Equally, if any differences exist between the two diagnostic groups in terms of the factor profiles, such differences would be of the same magnitude and direction in all the centres (centre versus diagnostic group interaction hypothesis). This hypothesis was *not rejected* by the results of

---

[1] A factor score F_i is a linear compound $F_i = b_{i1} x_1 + b_{i2} x_2 + \dots b_{ik} x_k$ of the original variables $x_1, x_2 \dots x_k$ where b_{ij} are weights computed in the analysis; k is the number of original variables on which the factor analysis was based. The scores have been normalized with a mean for the total study population equalling 0 and a standard deviation of 1. A negative mean factor score for a particular centre implies that the "expression" of the factor in that centre was weaker than the average for all centres combined.

Table 22. Mean factor scores (first 15 principal components) by centre and diagnostic group

Diagnostic group	Factor (principal component)	Field research centres					All FRCs
		Basle	Montreal	Nagasaki	Teheran	Tokyo	
Endogenous	1	0.449	0.480	0.620	0.094	-0.140	0.301
	2	0.218	0.003	0.037	-0.010	-0.020	0.045
	3	0.041	0.325	-0.717	-0.651	-0.204	-0.296
	4	0.385	-0.113	-0.293	-0.090	-0.135	0.054
	5	0.182	0.217	0.045	-0.140	0.001	0.054
	6	-0.244	0.194	-0.029	-0.683	-0.087	-0.166
	7	0.239	0.062	0.075	-0.042	0.199	0.116
	8	-0.065	-0.247	0.420	-0.846	0.601	0.082
	9	0.263	-0.284	0.340	-0.084	-0.487	-0.026
	10	-0.069	-0.310	0.095	0.591	-0.311	-0.011
	11	0.227	0.427	-0.070	0.045	-0.053	0.076
	12	0.151	-0.431	0.215	-0.421	-0.141	-0.070
	13	-0.217	-0.138	0.435	-0.001	-0.252	-0.002
	14	-0.180	0.046	0.114	0.261	-0.221	-0.009
	15	-0.131	-0.150	0.134	-0.187	0.052	-0.025
Psychogenic	1	-0.019	-0.224	-0.283	-0.880	-0.835	-0.398
	2	0.155	-0.097	-0.216	-0.151	-0.119	-0.041
	3	0.714	0.593	-0.395	-0.067	0.223	0.382
	4	0.500	0.377	-0.389	-0.288	-0.335	0.124
	5	0.030	-0.243	-0.390	-0.166	-0.192	-0.143
	6	0.422	0.354	0.608	-0.024	0.095	0.268
	7	-0.164	-0.202	-0.105	-0.011	0.199	-0.083
	8	0.267	-0.428	0.453	-0.530	0.310	-0.077
	9	0.221	0.235	-0.204	-0.137	-0.209	0.060
	10	0.173	-0.321	-0.174	0.241	0.268	0.047
	11	-0.269	-0.062	-0.110	-0.052	-0.061	-0.012
	12	0.360	-0.221	0.991	-0.099	0.054	0.871
	13	-0.362	-0.115	0.460	0.387	-0.432	-0.104
	14	-0.105	0.175	-0.256	0.195	-0.160	0.019
	15	0.116	-0.056	0.152	0.015	0.113	0.048

	Total (includes all patients)					
1	0.217	0.063	0.427	−0.431	−0.320	0.000
2	0.163	−0.061	0.000	−0.088	−0.053	0.000
3	0.407	0.544	−0.626	−0.347	−0.082	0.000
4	0.415	0.188	−0.306	−0.199	−0.196	0.000
5	0.185	−0.041	−0.012	−0.123	−0.054	0.000
6	0.074	0.290	0.039	−0.392	−0.033	0.000
7	0.008	−0.118	−0.032	−0.049	0.179	0.000
8	0.101	−0.371	0.433	−0.726	0.502	0.000
9	0.206	0.010	0.265	−0.110	−0.403	0.000
10	0.043	−0.288	0.091	0.301	−0.147	0.000
11	−0.043	0.189	−0.078	0.003	−0.055	0.000
12	0.212	−0.301	0.304	−0.234	−0.035	0.000
13	−0.305	−0.100	0.539	0.282	−0.316	0.000
14	−0.142	0.116	0.070	0.193	−0.190	0.000
15	−0.036	−0.058	0.141	−0.116	0.073	0.000

MANOVA ($P < 0.05$). In other words, differences in factor profiles of depression that could be found between the centres may not be due to the differences between subgroups of patients with endogenous and psychogenic depressions, which are represented in different proportions in the centres.

Hypothesis 2. There are no differences between the centres in terms of the 15-variate factor profiles of depressive patients. This hypothesis was *rejected* by the results of MANOVA at the level of $P < 0.0001$. The rejection of this hypothesis indicated that groups of patients in centres differed in regard to their average factor profiles. Pairwise comparisons of every possible pair of centres were carried out in respect of each of the 15 factors. Simultaneous confidence intervals were computed with a confidence coefficient of 95% and 99%. The results are presented in Table 23. "Simultaneous" confidence intervals mean that the confidence coefficient of 99% (or 95%) refers to all intervals simultaneously. With the exception of Basle and Teheran, which did not differ significantly in respect of the average factor profiles, there were significant differences in respect of one to three factors between all the other pairs of centres. All the differences between centres concerned Factors: 1 (anergia/retardation), 3 (abnormal personality), 4 (previous depressive episodes), 8 (socioeconomic status), 9 (sleep disturbance), 12 (hypochondriasis), and 13 (other symptoms). By factors, the differences between centres were as follows:

Factor 1 (anergia/retardation): *Basle* scores higher than *Teheran* and *Tokyo*, and *Nagasaki* higher than *Tokyo*.

Factor 3 (abnormal personality): *Basle* and *Montreal* score higher than *Nagasaki* and *Teheran*.

Factor 4 (previous depressive episodes): *Basle* scores higher than *Nagasaki*.

Factor 8 (socioeconomic status): *Basle* and *Tokyo* score higher than *Montreal*.

Factor 9 (sleep disturbance): *Nagasaki* scores higher than *Tokyo*.

Factor 12 (hypochondriasis): *Nagasaki* scores higher than *Montreal*.

Factor 13 (other symptoms): *Nagasaki* scores higher than *Tokyo*.

Generally, the differences that were found between centres in assessed symptom profiles and other characteristics of patients with depressive disorders are few, especially when each of the 10 possible pairs of centres could differ on every one and on any combination of the 15 factors. (It should be noted also that the emergence of significant differences due to chance, because of the large number of variables involved, was ruled out by the multivariate tests of significance and by the computation of simultaneous confidence intervals.) This indicates one of the following: (*a*) the groups of depressive patients in the study were relatively similar across the different centres; (*b*) potentially important differences between patient groups were not picked up by the rating instrument; or (*c*) factor analysis in these instances was not the method best suited to establishing differences and examining them.

Table 23. Results of two-way multivariate analysis of variance on 15-variate factor profiles by centre (only factors for which significant differences were demonstrated are shown)

	Montreal	Nagasaki	Teheran	Tokyo
Basle	No significant differences	3[a] (Abnormal personality) 4[b] (Previous depressive episodes) 13[a] (Other symptoms)	1[a] (Anergia/retardation) 3[a] (Abnormal personality) 8[a] (Socioeconomic status)	1[a] (Anergia/retardation)
Montreal		3[a] (Abnormal personality) 8[a] (Socioeconomic status) 12[b] (Hypochondriasis)	3[a] (Abnormal personality)	8[a] (Socioeconomic status)
Nagasaki			8[a] (Socioeconomic status)	1[b] (Anergia/retardation) 9[b] (Sleep disturbance) 13[a] (Other symptoms)
Teheran				8[a] (Socioeconomic status)

[a] Significant at the 0.01 level (multivariate test).
[b] Significant at the 0.05 level (multivariate test).

Differences between the diagnostic groups of endogenous and psychogenic depressive disorders: results of MANOVA and of discriminant function analysis on factor profiles and individual items

It having been established that it was statistically justified to assume that there was no interaction between centres and diagnostic groups (i.e., that patients with endogenous and with psychogenic depressions in each centre contributed similarly to the between-centre differences described in the preceding section), the next question was: have psychiatrists used the two diagnostic labels of endogenous and psychogenic depressive disorders in a consistent and appropriate way considering their diagnoses of all patients in the study?

Hypothesis 3. No differences exist between the diagnostic groups of endogenous and psychogenic depressive disorders in terms of 15-variate factor profiles. The results of MANOVA *reject* this hypothesis at the level of $P < 0.0001$—i.e., there are differences between the factor profiles of the two diagnostic groups. To identify the factors that contributed to these differences, again simultaneous confidence intervals were computed with confidence coefficients of 95% and 99%.

Factor 1 (anergia/retardation): Patients with endogenous depression score higher than patients with psychogenic depression ($P < 0.01$, multivariate test).

Factor 3 (abnormal personality): Patients with psychogenic depression score higher than patients with endogenous depression ($P < 0.01$, multivariate test).

Factor 6 (dejection): Patients with psychogenic depression score higher than patients with endogenous depression ($P < 0.05$). Since, however, this factor appeared to be less stable on internal replication than the other two, and since in addition the statistical significance of the difference is lower, Factor 6 will be disregarded in further discussion.

As the factors (principal components) describing the patients are orthogonal to each other, the main differences between the groups of patients classified as suffering from endogenous and psychogenic depressions can be presented in a simple graph (Fig. 6). The relative similarity of both endogenous depressives and psychogenic depressives in Basle and Montreal is as striking as the magnitude of the differences between the patients assessed in Tokyo and in Nagasaki. Endogenous depressions in Tokyo are closer to the psychogenic depressions than to the endogenous depressions in Nagasaki.

The next question was: which factors discriminate best between the diagnostic groups of endogenous and psychogenic depressions within the separate field research centres? To answer this question, discriminant function analysis was performed: (*a*) using scores for the 15 factors, and (*b*) using scores on each of the individual items of WHO/SADD.

Stepwise discriminant analysis was used to identify the subset of variables (items or factors) that would maximize the separation between the two diagnostic groups. Variables were entered into the analysis one at a time until the separation between the groups ceased to improve. As a first step of the analysis, the variables for which the means differed most in both diagnostic

Fig. 6. Differences between endogenous and psychogenic depressive disorders in terms of two orthogonal factors ($P = 0.01$, MANOVA)

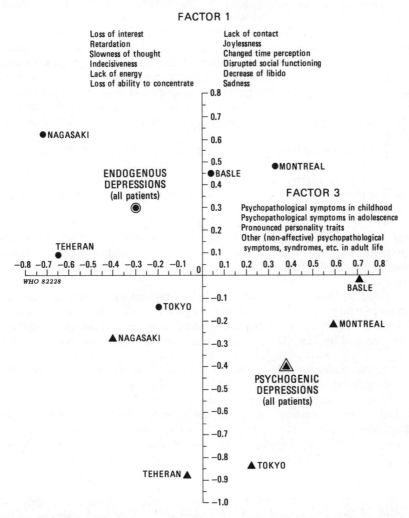

groups were entered first. Then the differences between the means in the two diagnostic groups were calculated for each of the remaining variables, eliminating all the effects of possible correlations with the variable already entered in the discriminant function. The variable for which those "conditional" means differed most was entered next into the analysis. Each time a variable was entered, the discriminant function was recomputed including the variable. The discriminant functions thus obtained, one for each diagnostic group, were used to calculate for every patient the probability that he/she belonged to the first or the second group, given each profile in terms of the variables (either factors or original items) already entered into the functions. Every patient was then assigned to the endogenous or the psychogenic depression group, depending on which probability was higher.

The discriminant function analysis can be considered successful if few cases are misclassified. If a large percentage of the patients is classified correctly (i.e., if the probabilities derived in the analysis assign them to their "source" group), it can be accepted that differences between the two groups do exist and that the set of discriminating variables has been selected correctly. The corresponding discriminant functions can be used to classify any new patient into the most likely diagnostic group on the basis of factor or item profile.

The best discriminatory factors were already identified as a result of the MANOVA: anergia/retardation (Factor 1), abnormal personality (Factor 3) and, to a limited degree, dejection (Factor 6) separate both diagnostic groups best. The technique of stepwise discriminant analysis was applied to assess the classification power of those factors.

As already indicated, by restricting the analysis to factors, some of the total information available is disregarded. To check whether items not represented by any of the 15 factors might have significant discriminatory power, stepwise discriminant analyses were also carried out on the original items.

Table 24 demonstrates that the factors discriminating best between the two diagnostic groups in the total study population (all centres combined) were 1, 3 and 6—i.e., the same factors for which differences between the two groups were identified by MANOVA. If only scores on these three factors are used to assign patients to the endogenous and the psychogenic groups, about 25% (i.e., every fourth patient) would be misclassified. If all the 15 factors are used, the misclassification rate would diminish only slightly. It is obvious that a classification procedure for patients on the basis of factor scores would be inadequate for practical purposes quite apart from its computational complexity. From a theoretical point of view, however, that it is possible to classify correctly the majority of patients on the basis of their factor scores suggests that the two diagnostic groups have distinct characteristics.

A more practical procedure, which is used by clinicians, is the classification of patients into two diagnostic groups on the basis of the presence or absence of specific items (symptoms or other characteristics) selected through clinical observation and considered to be associated with one or the other entity (or extreme on the phenomenological continuum, according to those who do not accept the categorial distinction between endogenous and psychogenic depressions). The patterns of symptoms, signs, and other characteristics supposed to distinguish endogenous from psychogenic depressive illnesses are likely to vary within certain limits from centre to centre and among individual clinicians. In spite of such variation, there seems to be general agreement that, for example, retarded depressions with diurnal fluctuations of mood (worse in the morning), sleep disorder (early awakening), emergence of characteristic delusions, etc., in the absence of a history of

Table 24. (A) Factors discriminating between the groups of patients with endogenous and psychogenic depressions: Results of stepwise discriminant function analysis

Factor	Basle		Montreal		Nagasaki		Teheran		Tokyo		All centres combined	
	Factor no.	Misclassification rate (%)	Factor no.	Misclassification rate (%)	Factor no.	Misclassification rate (%)	Factor no.	Misclassification rate (%)	Factor no.	Misclassification rate (%)	Factor no.	Misclassification rate (%)
Best discriminating factor	6	37.0	1	32.0	1	28.0	1	29.2	1	29.5	1	34.0
Second best	3	30.7	5	28.2	6	27.0	3	21.9	3	25.9	3	28.3
Third best	1	26.8	2	26.2	12	25.0	2	16.7	8	27.7	6	24.9
All 15 factors		23.6		24.3		13.0		17.7		21.4		23.6

(B) "Forced" discrimination and misclassification rates with use of Factors 1, 3 and 6 only

Factor no.	Basle	Montreal		Nagasaki		Teheran		Tokyo		All centres combined	
	Misclassification rate (%)	Factor no.	Misclassification rate (%)	Factor no.	Misclassification rate (%)	Factor no.	Misclassification rate (%)	Factor no.	Misclassification rate (%)	Factor no.	Misclassification rate (%)
6	37.0	1	32.0	1	28.0	1	29.2	1	29.5	1	34.0
3	30.7	3	34.0	3	27.0	3	21.9	3	25.9	3	28.3
1	26.8	6	33.0	6	27.0	6	18.7	6	26.8	6	24.9

Table 25. WHO/SADD items discriminating between the groups of patients with function

	Basle		Montreal		Nagasaki	
	Item	%mc[a]	Item	%mc	Item	%mc
Best	Age	29.9	Psychomotor retardation	30.1	Early awakening	23.0
2nd	Continual psychological stress	19.7	Age	31.1	Duration of present episode	26.0
3rd	History of affective disorder in relatives	16.5	Continual psychological stress	19.4	Marital status: separated	17.0
4th	Course of present episode	9.4	Delusions of guilt	18.4	Worse in the morning	11.0
5th	Disruption of social functioning	9.4	No. of years since 1st depressive episode	15.5	Continual psychological stress	6.0

[a] %mc = % Misclassified.

precipitating stress or events in patients who may have had previous affective illnesses and, in a proportion of cases, a family history of similar disorders, should be classified as endogenous. Likewise, depressive illnesses in persons who often display neurotic premorbid traits, arising in relation to psychological stress and characterized by more variable mood, absence of characteristic diurnal fluctuations (or feeling worse in the evening), sleep disturbance, delusions, etc. are usually classified as psychogenic.

The emergence of patterns of recognizable diagnostic stereotypes of the two groups of depressive disorders in the analysis may suggest that the analysis of the discriminative power of individual WHO/SADD items would be an exercise in tautology. This, however, is not the case, although psychiatrists undoubtedly use mental checklists in classifying patients. Firstly, these checklists may not be quite identical, either in item composition or in the weight attributed to individual items. Secondly, even if a stereotype of the disorder is adopted by a clinician, his actual diagnostic performance may deviate in unspecified ways from the algorithm of the stereotype. Thirdly, a substantial proportion of the patients are likely to present features not clearly related to either of the stereotypes, and diagnostic decisions about such patients have to be made *ad hoc*, on the basis of estimated similarity of the condition to one of the diagnostic stereotypes.

For this reason, it was of interest to see which WHO/SADD items contributed most to the discrimination between endogenous and psychogenic depressions in the individual centres regardless of whether such items are part of the explicit stereotype of the disorder. The results of the stepwise discriminant function analysis are presented in Table 25. Only the five best discriminating items are listed, along with the corresponding misclassification rates. Statistical significance tests were not carried out as many of the items endogenous and psychogenic depressions: Results of stepwise discriminant analysis

Teheran		Tokyo		All centres combined	
Item	%mc	Item	%mc	Item	%mc
Precipitating stress	31.2	Duration of present episode	18.7	Continual psychological stress	32.0
Psychopathological symptoms in adolescence	24.0	Course of present episode	13.4	Early awakening	29.0
Early awakening	20.8	Worse in the morning	11.6	Psychomotor retardation	25.1
Lack of contact	18.7	Lack of contact	11.6	Psychopathological symptoms in childhood	24.5
Worse in the morning	18.7	Pronounced traits of premorbid personality	9.8	No. of years since 1st depressive episode	22.7

entering the analyses are of the categorial type and do not conform to the mathematical assumptions underlying such tests. However, the practical significance of their discriminatory power may be assessed by their "ability" to classify patients correctly into diagnostic groups. It could be shown that including more than three (in some centres five) variables did not decrease substantially the number of misclassified patients.

The table shows that the five "best" discriminating items varied from centre to centre, although all of them have a *prima facie* validity in the sense that they can be linked to the clinical stereotypes of endogenous and psychogenic depressive illnesses. It is also impressive that with only five items, the majority of the patients could be classified correctly (the rate of misclassification being as low as 6% in one centre, 9.4% and 9.8% in another type, and 15.5% and 18.1% in the remaining two centres). In most of the centres, symptoms of the index episode appeared to be less important in the differentiation between the two diagnostic groups than items describing aspects of psychiatric or personal history and demographic items such as age.

On the whole, the results of discriminant function analysis on individual items indicate that psychiatrists in the different centres used similar stereotypes for classifying depressive patients into an endogenous and a psychogenic group but the relative importance (weight) attached to individual items varied between centres (and probably between clinicians in the centres). Although the results of this analysis cannot be interpreted as supporting or not supporting the validity of the classification of depressive conditions into an endogenous and a psychogenic group (this issue will be approached when follow-up data become available), they at least demonstrate that patients can be assigned to such groups in a fairly consistent manner on the basis of specifiable diagnostic criteria.

Summary and conclusions

To group the various characteristics of patients with depressive disorders assessed in the five centres into units that would make it possible to examine similarities or dissimilarities between the centres and between the two major diagnostic groups (endogenous and psychogenic), the data related to 66 SADD items for a total of 573 patients were pooled and factor-analysed using the technique of principal component analysis.

The first 15 orthogonal factors that emerged explained about 50% of the variance. These factors were given a clinical interpretation above in the section entitled "Factors describing the total study population (all centres combined)".

An internal replication of the analysis (carried out on a systematic sample that included every second patient) confirmed the stability of 13 of the 15 factors (the exceptions were Factors 6 and 12).

The groups of patients in the different centres were then compared on the basis of results of two-way multivariate analysis of variance. Three conclusions were drawn from this analysis:

(1) The differences that might exist between the average factor profiles of patients in the separate research centres could not be explained by the presence of differing proportions of endogenous and psychogenic disorders in the centres.

(2) There were significant differences (overall significance level $P < 0.01$) between the averaged factor profiles in all possible pairs of centres except for the pair Basle–Montreal. Some of these differences are clearly ascribable to nosocomial factors (e.g., that all patients in Basle were treated as inpatients and may thus be patients with a different severity of illness). The differences concerned the centre scores for Factors 1, 3, 8, and 13 in more than one pairwise comparison, and Factors 4, 9, and 12, each in one of the pairwise comparisons. Patients in Basle had higher scores on anergia/retardation than patients in Teheran and Tokyo, and patients in Nagasaki scored higher than patients in Tokyo on the same factor. Scores on abnormal personality were higher in Basle and Montreal than in Nagasaki and Teheran.

(3) Considering the many ways in which factor profiles of patient groups in the different centres could differ from each other, the actually observed number of significant differences was relatively small. This suggests one of the following possibilities: (a) the patients in the study were a relatively homogeneous group; (b) potentially important differences were not picked up by the rating schedule; or (c) the factor analysis is not sufficient for this analysis. The second possibility concerns the validity of the rating instrument and procedure; this will be evaluated as results of the follow-up study on the same patients become available. All that can be stated on the basis of initial assessment data is that the items included in the schedule can discriminate between diagnostic subtypes of depression, which suggests that its construct validity is acceptable.

The ability of factors and individual WHO/SADD items to discriminate between diagnostic groups of depressive disorders (using as a criterion the psychiatrists' classification of patients into an endogenous and a psychogenic depression category) was tested by means of multivariate analysis of variance (MANOVA) and stepwise discriminant function analysis.

Results of MANOVA on factor profiles demonstrated that the groups of patients diagnosed as suffering from endogenous or psychogenic depressive illnesses differed significantly from one another in terms of only two orthogonal factors: Factor 1 (anergia/retardation) and Factor 3 (abnormal personality). Patients with endogenous depression tended to have higher scores on anergia/retardation and lower scores on abnormal personality. Patients with psychogenic depression tended to have higher scores on abnormal personality and lower scores on anergia/retardation.

Discriminant function analysis indicated that endogenous and psychogenic depressive illnesses could be separated in terms of mean scores for Factors 1 and 3 with misclassification rates ranging from 21.9% to 34.0% (average 28.3%) in the different centres. This indicates that, regardless of the predictive validity of the distinction between them, the two diagnostic groups could be clearly differentiated in the study. This could be interpreted as evidence in favour of the construct validity of the phenomenological distinction between endogenous and psychogenic depressions.

The individual WHO/SADD items that discriminated best between the two types of depression varied somewhat from centre to centre, but they all belonged to the clinical stereotypes of the endogenous and psychogenic depressions proposed by supporters of this classification. Moreover, it appears that these discriminating items were used consistently in the centres, since the misclassification rates obtained with only 5 items were as low as 6.0–9.8% in three centres and 15.5% and 18.7% in the remaining two. In all centres combined, the items discriminating best between endogenous and psychogenic depression were: presence of continual psychological stress and history of psychopathological symptoms in childhood—characteristic of psychogenic depression; and psychomotor retardation, early awakening, and a history of past depressive episodes (more precisely a great number of years since the first depressive episode)—characteristic of endogenous depression.

6. Summary and conclusions

Although prevalence figures vary from study to study, and from one investigator to another, there is at present little doubt that depressive disorders occur in all parts of the world and that depressive patients constitute a significant proportion of all people who need or seek mental health care. An important number of such patients approach general health care services, where their depression often remains unrecognized.

There is little doubt, either, that most depressive patients receive no treatment although there are effective therapies and secondary prevention measures. In addition to the extreme scarcity of mental health care resources, especially in the developing world, there are several specific obstacles to the timely treatment of depressive patients. Firstly, the medical profession, health administrators, and the general public are insufficiently aware of the means of treating depressive illnesses and preventing their recurrence. Secondly, the epidemiological data base is insufficient to allow a systematic planning of care for depressive patients, and there are no widely accepted methods of assessment and diagnosis that would produce such a data base. Thirdly, a lack of a common language among investigators and clinicians who deal with depressive disorders prevents a wider sharing of information, and makes it difficult to carry out comparative or cross-disciplinary investigations that would further our knowledge about the epidemiology, pathogenesis, and treatment of depressive disorders.

The present study, in which 573 patients with depressive disorders were selected and assessed in a uniform and standardized way by psychiatrists at five collaborating field research centres in four countries, is an effort at overcoming the third of these obstacles. Standardized methods of assessment and diagnosis that could be applied across cultures would help to overcome the first two obstacles.

The study had three principal aims: (a) to collect comparable information on groups of depressive patients at the different centres in order to increase knowledge about cross-cultural similarities or differences in the clinical picture, course and outcome, treatment and social impact of depressive conditions;

(b) to design relatively simple standard instruments and procedures for case-finding and for a clinical assessment of depressive patients in different cultural settings; and (c) to establish a network of research centres in different cultures capable of carrying out joint studies of depressive disorders and training investigators interested in standardized case-finding, assessment, and diagnostic techniques.

The initial phase of the project, which is described in the present report, achieved the second and third aims and provided some of the baseline data needed to achieve the first.

The field research centres that formed the network for the present study were attached to academic departments of psychiatry or to mental hospitals in Basle (Switzerland), Montreal (Canada), Nagasaki (Japan), Teheran (Iran), and Tokyo (Japan). They were selected because all had done interesting studies of depression, had on their staff well-trained, motivated investigators, and presented a range of different socioeconomic conditions and cultures.

Each centre defined a catchment area from which all patients to be included in the study were drawn. A comparison of some of the general characteristics of the catchment areas (Chapter 2) indicated both similarities and differences among them. They were similar in being exclusively or predominantly urban. Four were highly industrialized and one (Teheran) rapidly industrializing. There were important differences, however. Three (Basle, Montreal, and Teheran) had sizeable proportions of immigrant or indigenous cultural minorities, and the two in Japan had ethnically homogeneous populations. They also differed with regard to general medical and mental health care, Teheran having the least and Basle the most developed network of health and psychiatric services.

No attempt was made in this initial phase of the study to explore systematically the sociological, economic, and cultural aspects of the catchment areas, and their possible relation to the characteristics of depressive disorders identified in them (an assessment of selected social and cultural variables is being made in the follow-up study of the patients).

The results of the study lead to three groups of conclusions: (a) on the applicability and reliability of the instruments; (b) on the characteristics of the groups of patients included in the study; and (c) on the nature and classification of depressive disorders.

(1) Conclusions about the applicability and reliability of the instruments

Two instruments were designed and tested during the initial phase of the study: a screening instrument (WHO Depression Screen) and a WHO Schedule for Standardized Assessment of Depressive Disorders (WHO/SADD).

The screen is a simple checklist of inclusion and exclusion criteria that can be used by a psychiatrist, a psychologist, or a general practitioner for a very brief clinical interview with the patient. Its extensive testing on a total of 1208 patients attending the psychiatric services at the five centres indicated that in the hands of a trained observer it could help to select probable cases of depression with a high specificity (9.6% false positives) and a somewhat lower sensitivity (14.2% false negatives). A high specificity qualifies the screening instrument as particularly suitable for selecting homogeneous patient series for detailed clinical or biological investigations. The sensitivity of the screen will need to be increased, however, if it is to be used in epidemiological studies. Data being collected in a current study in which patients attending general practitioners' clinics are being screened for depressive disorders will permit the assessment of the screen's applicability to non-psychiatric patients.

The WHO Schedule for Standardized Assessment of Depressive Disorders (WHO/SADD) was designed to be a relatively simple but sufficiently comprehensive instrument that could uniformly elicit and record depressive symptomatology and previous history, that would be easily adaptable to individual interviewing styles, and that would not be time-consuming. It was designed in a way that differed from the usual method (of reducing and collapsing an initially large pool of items) around a "core" set of items on which there was wide consensus that they reflected essential features of depressive disorders and could discriminate between major subtypes of depression. Items related to less typical symptoms and signs of depression were added sparingly, and several open-ended ratings on "other symptoms" were included to provide for recording rare or centre-specific symptoms. It was constructed in a series of stages, with extensive discussion of its content by all the investigators. A glossary with brief definitions and guidelines for rating was compiled as a companion to the schedule. It was translated from English into German, Japanese, and Farsi and back-translated into English repeatedly until semantic equivalence was achieved.

After an initial period of training and trial use, the investigators at each centre rated a number of patients jointly to assess the reliability of the method. Intercentre reliability exercises took place during every exchange of visits by the investigators, and in the intervals between meetings through exchanges of videotapes, audiotapes, and films.

The general impression of the investigators was that the WHO/SADD schedule was easy to master, flexible enough to be adapted to the psychiatrist's routine method of clinical examination, and acceptable to the patients. No difficulties were reported with the acceptability of item contents in the different cultural settings.

The reliability of assessments made using the schedule, as indicated by the agreement ratio and the "probabilities of correct rating" (π), was relatively high within the individual centres and acceptable in the between-centre exercises. There were certain differences in the reliability of its different parts. Thus, the reliability of the sociodemographic description was highest (the agreement rate for the items was between 0.95 and 1.0 and π reached 98%), and that of the symptom section next highest (average agreement rate on symptoms 0.92, and π 96%). The somewhat lower reliability of the items describing the psychiatric history (intraclass correlations ranging from 0.34 to 0.98 and π 86–98%) was mainly due to the difficulty in estimating the number of previous manic episodes and the number of years since the first manic episode. Similar difficulties arose in assessing the onset of the present episode.[1]

---

[1] The item was eliminated in the 5th revision of the WHO/SADD.

Concerning the comprehensiveness of the instrument—i.e., the extent to which the items cover the whole spectrum of symptoms and signs of functional depressive illnesses—the analysis of the responses of psychiatrists to the open-ended items on "other symptoms" provides certain clues. Firstly, it appeared that very few "culture-specific" or "centre-specific" symptoms were identified in the patient groups at the different centres. This finding may be due to the nature of services from which the patients were selected and without an epidemiological investigation it is not likely that an answer can be given to the question of the frequency of such symptoms. Secondly, at all centres there were several categories of symptoms and signs that were recorded consistently in a sizeable minority of the patients and might merit inclusion in a future, more comprehensive version of SADD. These categories of symptoms and signs included: (a) somatic complaints and signs, (b) obsessional symptoms, (c) phobias and panic attacks, (d) depersonalization and derealization, (e) auditory hallucinations, (f) fatigue, (g) sexual dysfunctions, (h) hysterical phenomena, and (i) side-effects of drugs.

(2) Conclusions about the characteristics of the patients included in the study

If the study patients can be accepted as typical of the usual caseload of the five centres, then it can be said that the patients who seek psychiatric treatment for a depressive illness in the five study areas are strikingly similar in many respects.

Allowing for some variations, the male patients tended to be young adults, and most of the females were in early middle age. At every centre except Tokyo female patients outnumbered males. Occupationally, the largest single group were housewives. Most of the patients were married and, except in Teheran, were of a medium economic status and a fairly high level of education.

For almost half the patients the current depressive illness was not the first depressive episode, but only a small proportion (6.8%) had had manic attacks earlier. Upon inclusion in the study and initial assessment, 56.7% were given diagnoses that could be classified into an *endogenous* group of disorders, and 37.2% into a *psychogenic* depression group. The endogenous depression category was more numerous at all centres except Montreal.

With regard to symptomatology, the patients at all centres exhibited a "core" of depressive symptoms that were present in 76–100% in both diagnostic groups: sadness, joylessness, anxiety, tension, lack of energy, loss of interest, loss of ability to concentrate, and ideas of insufficiency, inadequacy, or worthlessness. In contrast to these most frequent symptoms, only one-third had hypochondriacal ideas or preoccupations, and only 2–5% depressive delusions of any kind. About 40% had "other" symptoms of the type listed in (1) above and an equal proportion had various somatic symptoms and signs. Only a few symptoms appeared with markedly different frequency at the different centres. Examples are psychomotor agitation (generally rare but rather frequent in Teheran) and feelings of guilt and self-reproach (68% in Basle but only 32% in Teheran). Over half had suicidal thoughts, with some variation across the centres. There was a remarkable absence of culture-specific symptoms—i.e., manifestations that would not fit the classical descriptive phenomenology of depressive disorders.

It was not possible to range patients along a continuum of "severity" (since no validation criteria for a measure of severity were available in this cross-section of depressive symptomatology) but if the clinical manifestations of anergic-retarded and "vital" depression are considered as possible indices of greater severity, then more patients in Nagasaki, Basle, and Montreal would have severe depression than patients in Teheran and Tokyo. As a group (regardless of subtype diagnosis), depressive patients in Basle and Montreal tended more frequently to manifest personality abnormalities and to have a previous history of nonaffective psychiatric disturbances.

Although the symptom profiles of the depressive disorders were very similar at the different centres, the management of the patients by the psychiatric services differed widely. While all patients in Basle, and almost all in Montreal, were inpatients at the time of initial assessment, most of the patients at the other three centres were being treated as outpatients. Most were having drug treatment, which in a minority was combined with some form of psychotherapy. Electroconvulsive treatment was used in only a few cases.

These results leave no doubt that in the different cultures represented in the study there were patients suffering from functional depressive illnesses who had a very similar past history and symptom profile of the index episode. However, the existence of such a nuclear group of depressive disorders, in which no marked cultural variation could be observed, does not rule out the existence of many other "atypical" or "culture-specific" syndromes of depression for which different case-finding and assessment procedures would have to be designed.

(3) Conclusions concerning the nature and classification of depressive disorders

Utilizing principal component analysis, it was possible to condense and reduce the characteristics of the patients included in the study to a set of factors of which the first 15 explained about 50% of the variation in the data. Most of these factors could easily be interpreted clinically. Factor profiles of groups of patients, constructed from the scores on the first 15 principal components, were compared using a two-way multivariate analysis of variance, and rigorous tests for statistical significance of the differences were applied. There were relatively few significant differences between the patients at the different centres—a fact that underscores the conclusions outlined in the foregoing section. There were two significant differences between the factor profiles of patients assigned to the endogenous depression and the psychogenic depression groups. The endogenous depressives scored higher on the factor "anergia-retardation" and the psychogenic depressives scored higher on the factor "abnormal personality". These two major factors can be represented as two orthogonal dimensions that define the factorial space of the two classificatory concepts. Stepwise discriminant function analysis on both factor scores and individual items showed that the two diagnostic groups could be differentiated reliably although many of their characteristics overlapped.

These findings raise two questions: one of a somewhat theoretical nature and one of some practical consequence. The first question concerns the nosological status of the distinction between endogenous and psychogenic depressive disorders. While the validity of this distinction can be established only with reference to independent criteria (e.g., biological markers, follow-up data on course and outcome), there is sufficient evidence from the multivariate statistical analysis of the study material that the two constructs (endogenous and psychogenic) can be supported by data. At the same time, however, there is evidence that the two groups of patients identified on the basis of these constructs cannot be fully separated. This means that, on a basis of symptoms, the syndromes of endogenous and psychogenic depressions could be conceptualized as two overlapping clusters or extremes on a continuum rather than as two mutually exclusive categories.

The second question concerns the possibility of discriminating reliably between the two syndromes in everyday clinical practice, in view of the possible implications of such a discrimination for the rational choice of treatment and management. The results of the stepwise discriminant function analysis provided a clear answer to this question, at least with regard to the patients and centres included in the study. It turned out that at three centres 91.2–94.0% of the patients could be classified into the groups of endogenous and psychogenic depression on the basis of information about only five WHO/SADD items.[1] For the remaining two centres the proportion was somewhat lower: 81.3–84.5%, and for the study population as a whole it was 77.3%. The five best discriminating items, however, varied from centre to centre. For all patients in the study they included two symptoms of the present state (early awakening and psychomotor retardation) and three history items (continuing psychological stress, history of psychopathological symptoms in childhood, and number of years since the first depressive episode). At the separate centres, some of the best discriminating items (e.g., age, marital status, disruption of social functioning, lack of contact) were not among those that usually described the diagnostic stereotypes of the two types of depression. These findings suggest that there were no truly pathognomonic symptoms the presence or absence of which would unequivocally place a patient in one or the other diagnostic group, but rather that patients were classified on the basis of clusters of characteristics within which some but not others were given greater weight by different diagnosticians and at different centres. The practical consequences of the observed misclassification rates (i.e., the percentages of patients whom the analysis assigns to one or other diagnostic group) for treatment and management will be evaluated when follow-up data on the course and outcome and the response to treatment of the two subtypes of depressive disorders become available.

---

[1] As stressed before, the findings suggest that physicians make their distinctions among diagnoses on the basis of a small number of symptoms, which are perhaps "cores" or "nodes" of clusters.

Directions for further work

The results of the initial phase of the study should permit further developments in several directions. These include research, instrument development and training in their use, and transfer of information.

Concerning research, studies are now needed to answer the questions about the predictive validity of the differences found between patients in the two diagnostic groups. For this purpose a follow-up study was considered necessary to attempt to reassess as many as possible of the original patients five years after the initial assessment. A trial follow-up study has been carried out at one of the centres (Teheran) with encouraging results concerning feasibility, and the centres have then undertaken a follow-up investigation in which course and outcome, treatment, and social implications of the depressive disorders will be evaluated.

Further, an epidemiological study has been initiated by the centres to determine the frequency and clinical features of depressive disorders in patients seeking care in general health services. This study would also permit an evaluation of the effectiveness of case-finding for depressive conditions that general physicians can undertake, and provide a basis for training programmes for general practitioners and other health personnel.

Various links to biological research in depression are being made both at some of the collaborating centres and between them and other centres, especially as regards studies on biological markers (e.g., colour blindness) and mechanisms of treatment responses.

The instruments developed in the study have been adopted by investigators at several other centres for use in a broad spectrum of studies focusing on epidemiological and social aspects of depressive disorders. The centres that have participated in the study provide training in the use of the instruments that the study produced and assist other centres in investigations in which the instruments are being used. The WHO/SADD schedule has already been translated into several other languages (Bulgarian, Hindi, Polish). The availability of the schedules and glossary is a prerequisite for an effective transfer of information about depressive disorders in different sociocultural settings.

Whatever the results of these subsequent developments, the present study has already contributed to the achievement of two important objectives of WHO's work. The first is the strengthening of the capacity of countries to carry out research, to train their own research workers, and to investigate problems of public health importance. The second is the building of bridges between investigators, leading to the sharing of resources and the pooling of knowledge—a much needed outcome, if mental health sciences and practice are to contribute to better health care.

REFERENCES

BROWN, G. W. & HARRIS, T. (1978) *Social origins of depression*, London, Tavistock.

COPPEN, A. ET AL. (1978) Amitriptyline plasma-concentration and clinical effect. *Lancet*, 1: 63.

CRAIF, T. J. & VAN NATTA, P. A. (1978) Current medication use and symptoms of depression in a general population. *American journal of psychiatry*, 135: 9.

GERMAN, A. G. (1972) Aspects of clinical psychiatry in subsaharan Africa. *British journal of psychiatry*, 121: 461.

GERSHON, E. F. ET AL. (1980) A collaborative study of genetic linkage of bipolar manic-depressive illness and red/green colorblindness. *Acta psychiatrica scandinavica*, 61: 319.

GUILFORD, S. P. & FRUCHTER, B. (1973) *Fundamental statistics in psychology and education*, Tokyo, McGraw-Hill.

JABLENSKY, A. ET AL. (1981) Characteristics of depressive patients contacting psychiatric services in four cultures. *Acta psychiatrica scandinavica*, 63: 367.

KATSCHING, H. ET AL. (1980) Psychiatric case identification in general practice: self-rating versus interview. *Acta psychiatrica scandinavica*, 62, Supplement 285.

KENDELL, R. E. (1976) The classification of depression: a review of contemporary confusion. *British journal of psychiatry*, 129: 15.

KIELHOLZ, P. (1979) Le concept de la dépression masquée. *L'encéphale*, 5: 459.

LEHMANN, H. E. (1977) Classification of depressive states. *Canadian Psychiatric Association Journal*, 22: 381.

MELLINGER, G. D. ET AL. (1978) Psychic distress, life crisis and use of psycho-therapeutic medications, *Archives of general psychiatry*, 35: 1045.

POLDINGER, W. (1974) Enquiries on depression in everyday practice. In: Kielholz, P., ed., *Depression in everyday practice*, Bern, Huber.

REISBY, N. ET AL. (1977) Imipramine: clinical effects and pharmacokinetic variability. *Psychopharmacology*, 54: 263.

SARTORIUS, N. (1973) Culture and the epidemiology of depression. *Psychiatrica neurologia neurochirurgia*, 76: 479.

SARTORIUS, N. (1979) Research on affective psychoses within the framework of the WHO programme. In: Schon, M. & Strömgren, E., ed., *Origin, prevention and treatment of affective disorders*, London, Academic Press.

SARTORIUS, N. ET AL. (1980) Preliminary communication. WHO Collaborative Study: assessment of depressive disorders. *Psychological medicine*, 10: 743.

SHEPHERD, M. (1979) Approche épidémiologique de la dépression. *L'encéphale*, 5: 419.

TAKAHASHI, R. ET AL. (1979) Comparison of efficacy of amoxapine and imipramine in a multiclinic double-blind study using the WHO schedule for a standard assessment of patients with depressive disorders. *Journal of international medical research*, 7: 1.

WILSON, J. M. G. & JUNGNER, G. (1968) *Principles and practice of screening for disease*, Geneva, World Health Organization (Public Health Papers No. 34).

WORLD HEALTH ORGANIZATION (1973) *Report of the international pilot study of schizophrenia*, Vol. 1, Geneva, World Health Organization.

WORLD HEALTH ORGANIZATION (1974) *Suicide and attempted suicide*, Geneva, World Health Organization (Public Health Papers No. 58).

WORLD HEALTH ORGANIZATION (1978) *Mental disorders: glossary and guide to their classification in accordance with the Ninth Revision of the International Classification of Diseases*, Geneva, World Health Organization.

WORLD HEALTH ORGANIZATION (1979) *Schizophrenia: An international follow-up study*, Chichester, Wiley.

Annex 1

Notes on the concept of reliability

A widely accepted definition of reliability is based on the assumption that the measured or rated score x_m of a variable is additively composed of the true score x_r and an error increment x_e (i.e., $x_m = x_r + x_e$) where the "true" score is the genuine value of whatever is being measured, "the value we should obtain if we had a perfect instrument applied under ideal conditions" (Guilford & Fruchter[1]). The error component is assumed to occur independently and at random, which implies that a psychiatrist interviewing and rating the symptoms of a series of patients rates with the same accuracy for the first patient as for the last one. Furthermore, the error components x_e should not correlate with the true values x_r, which means that the rating is done with the same reliability for patients who have the symptom as for those who do not have it. Finally, the above model requires that different raters measure with similar reliability. This assumption in many cases is fulfilled at most only approximately. Denoting by σ_r^2 and σ_m^2 the variances of the true and measured scores respectively, the reliability coefficient r^2 is then defined by $r^2 = \sigma_r^2/\sigma_m^2$—i.e., the reliability of the set of measurements x_m equals the proportion of their variance that is true variance.

In practice, however, x_r and x_e are not directly measurable, and hence σ_r^2 and σ_m^2 are not known. Therefore, to assess the reliability of the rating procedures, a series of patients may be assessed simultaneously and independently by two (or more) observers.

If two psychiatrists rate a series of patients with regard to a symptom or any other characteristic, three correlations may be distinguished (see Fig. A1): the correlation r_{r1} between the series of measurements of rater 1 and the true score, analogously r_{r2} for rater 2, and finally, the correlation r_{12} between the measurements of raters 1 and 2.

For characteristics measurable on a continuous scale, such as age, r_{12} can be calculated as a Pearson's or as an intraclass correlation coefficient. The square r_{r1}^2 of r_{r1}, as a coefficient of determination, quantifies the proportion of

---

[1] Guilford S. P. & Fruchter, B. (1973) *Fundamental statistics in psychology and education.* Tokyo, McGraw-Hill.

Fig. A1. Model of rating for dichotomous variables. Correlations r_{r1} and r_{r2}, i.e., between real value x_r and measurement x_m of rater 1 and 2 respectively, and correlation r_{12} between measurements of raters 1 and 2. Probability π_1 that the first rater's measurement x_{m1} is the true value x_r; probability π_2 that the second rater's measurement x_{m2} is the true value; agreement ratio a of both raters' measurements.

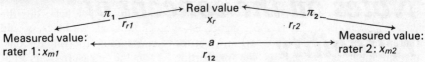

the total variance of the first rater's measurements that is true variance. Hence, by definition, r_{r1}^2 is the reliability of the instrument as used by rater 1 in the given situation. It can be shown that the directly measurable correlation r_{12} between the observations of the two raters is functionally related to the indices of reliability r_{r1} and r_{r2} of the rating instrument as used by the first and second rater respectively. Since the index of reliability is the square root of the reliability, $r_{12} = \sqrt{r_{r1}\, r_{r2}}$, i.e., the correlation between the measurements of the observers is the geometric mean of their indices of reliability. If both raters have the same reliabilities it follows that the reliability of the measurements is given by the correlation between the measurements of both observers. Therefore, a natural indicator of reliability in the case of variables of the continuous type (e.g., age, number of previous episodes,[1] etc.) would be Pearson's coefficient of correlation calculated on the basis of the ratings of both psychiatrists participating in a reliability exercise. The questions then arise: which is the first and which the second observation. The problem is met by entering in the calculation both possible pairs, i.e., those obtained by taking each psychiatrist first. A coefficient of this kind is called intraclass correlation coefficient. It is used to quantify reliability in relation to continuous variables.

In principle, the definition of reliability of measurements given by Guilford—i.e., the proportion of variance that is true variance—holds equally for variables of the continuous type as for the dichotomous or polychotomous characteristics. However, for dichotomies (e.g., symptoms that may be either present or absent) the variance strongly depends on the frequency of occurrence of the specific symptom. This is demonstrated by the following example: a psychiatrist may be able to measure correctly the presence or absence of a certain symptom in a clinical interview in, say, 90% of the cases. The prevalence of the symptom in a certain patient group may be 5%—i.e., in 95% of the patients the symptom is absent. It can be calculated that the proportion of the variance that is true variance (i.e., the reliability of the measurements) in this instance would be 0.24. However, if the same psychiatrist, who is assumed to rate correctly with a probability of 90%, assesses a group of patients in which the proportion of subjects who do and do not have the symptom is equal (i.e., 50%), the reliability would be 0.64.

---

[1] Obviously, "number of previous episodes" is not a continuous variable. However, being an ordinal scale variable with many possible equidistant levels, it is treated as continuous.

In many cases it is undesirable to work with a coefficient of reliability whose numerical value depends cn the distribution of the variable under consideration in the patient population. In the above example, one would tend intuitively to describe the reliability of the rating procedure as 90% or 0.9—i.e., as the probability that the psychiatrist rates correctly—regardless of whether the symptom is present in only 5% or in 50% of the patients to be rated. A natural modification of Guilford's definition of reliability, which better fits the case of dichotomous, or, more generally, polychotomous variables, would therefore be: the reliability of any set of dichotomous (polychotomous) measurement is defined as the proportion π of the measurements that are correct measurements, or, equivalently, as the probability π that the measurement is correct.

Again, like r^2, π is not directly measurable. However, if in a two-rater reliability exercise two observers rate independently and simultaneously a group of patients, their agreement a can be calculated directly, analogously to the correlation r_{12} between the measurements of the first and second rater in the case of continuous variables. It can be shown that there is a relation between the measurable agreement ratio a of both raters' measurements and the reliability π_1 and π_2. If it can be assumed that the reliabilities of both psychiatrists' measurements are equal (or at least similar), then π-values can be calculated directly on the basis of the agreement ratio, in the same way as in the case of continuous variables, where the reliability of the measurements equals the square root of the correlation between the measurements of both observers. It may further be shown that a π-value of 0.5 signifies that the rating procedure is not reliable since the probability of the rating being correct or wrong is the same. The highest possible numerical value of π is 1.

If the assumption that both psychiatrists measure with equal reliability is unrealistic, the agreement ratio a can be used to estimate an average reliability for both raters. For continuous variables this average reliability is the geometric mean of the individual reliabilities. For dichotomous items the calculation of the average π-value is based upon the amount by which the individual π-value exceeds 0.5, i.e., the value of random judgement. This increment is the geometric mean of the increments of the individual π-values.[1]

In this study reliability for dichotomous and polychotomous items has been expressed in terms of π. The computation of π is based on the agreement ratio a of two observers.[2] Therefore the two-rater agreement ratio is also presented in most tables and graphs. In addition, the φ coefficient (for dichotomous variables) or the coefficient of contingency C (for polychotomous items) will be shown. If in the same interview the psychiatrist who conducted the interview is defined to be rater 1 and the observer defined to be rater 2, the result of such an interview in regard to a specific symptom may be summarized

---

[1] The average reliability is related to the individual values π_1 and π_2 of raters 1 and 2 respectively by the formula

$$\pi = 0.5 + \sqrt{(\pi_1 - 0.5)(\pi_2 - 0.5)}$$

[2] The agreement ratio for a particular symptom is defined as the number of ratings for which the raters achieved agreement divided by the total number of ratings.

Table A1

Symptom		Rater 2	
		absent	present
Rater 1	absent	*aa*	*ap*
	present	*pa*	*pp*

in a contingency table of the format shown in Table A1, in which *aa* is the number of agreements on symptom absence, *pp* on symptom presence, etc. If good agreement between both raters is achieved, (*aa* + *pp*) should be high in comparison with the disagreements (*ap* + *pa*). If χ^2 is calculated for the above table in the usual way, φ is given by $\varphi = \sqrt{\chi^2/N}$ where N is the total number of ratings (i.e., *aa* + *pp* + *ap* + *pa*). In the polychotomous case (more than two alternative outcomes of the rating) the coefficient of contingency C is computed by $C = \sqrt{\chi^2/(N + \chi^2)}$.

φ and C are product moment correlation coefficients like the intraclass correlation coefficient r. The numerical value of these coefficients is 0 if the measurements are not reliable; it is 1 if the assessment is possible without error. On the other hand, the π-value is measured on a scale between 0.5 and 1.0. To compare the numerical values of φ, C and r with those of π, a transformation $\varphi' = (\varphi + 1)/2$ etc. is recommended. After this transformation φ', C' and r', too, are dimensioned to vary between 0.5 and 1.0 only.

Reliability of patient assessment with WHO/SADD

(Supplementary statistical tables to Chapter 3)

Table A2. Reliability expressed in terms of two-rater agreement ratio *a* and probability π

Sociodemographic variable	Two-rater agreement ratio	ppi (π)
Age	—	1.00
Sex	1.00	1.00
Residence	0.99	0.99
Patient's status	0.98	0.99
Marital status	0.97	0.98
Employment	0.98	0.99
Intensity of work	0.95	0.98
Highest level of education	—	0.93
Economic status	0.95	0.98

Table A3. Correlation coefficients by centre for "Highest level of education"

	Basle	Montreal	Nagasaki	Teheran	Tokyo	All centres
Intracentre correlation coefficient	1.00	0.86	0.41	1.00	1.00	0.75
Transformed value	1.00	0.93	0.71	1.00	1.00	0.88

Table A4. Intracentre reliability exercise: Percentage positive ratings of symptoms and signs

Symptom	% rated present
1. Sadness	95
2. Joylessness	93
3. Hopelessness, inability to enjoy	80
4. Anxiety	83
5. Tension	79
6. Aggression, irritability	57
7. Lack of energy	91
8. Disruption of social functioning	87
9. Slowness or retardation of thought	73
10. Indecisiveness	74
11. Loss of interest	90
12. Loss of ability to concentrate	87
13. Change of perception of time	72
14. Feelings of guilt and self-reproach	62
15. Ideas of insufficiency, inadequacy and worthlessness, lack of self-confidence	89
16. Hypochondriasis	28
17. Ideas of impoverishment	35
18. Suicidal ideas	68
19. ideas of persecution and self-reference	35
20. Delusions of guilt	6
21. Delusions of hypochondriasis	3
22. Delusions of impoverishment and nihilism	2
23. Other delusions	0
24. Psychomotor retardation	77
25. Psychomotor agitation	46
26. Lack of contact	67
27. Worse in the morning	58
28. Worse in the evening	15
29. Decrease of libido	67
30. Early awakening	57
31. Inability to fall asleep	72
32. Fitful, restless sleep	71
33. Lack of appetite	73
34. Change of body weight	58
35. Constipation	54
36. Feelings of pressure or pain	60
37. Other somatic signs and symptoms	46
38. Other symptoms	38
39. Other symptoms	22

Past history items

40. History of psychiatric disorder in relatives (affective)	28
41. History of psychiatric disorder in relatives (general)	29
42. Early separation	32
43. Stressful events in childhood	23
44. Psychopathological symptoms in childhood	12
45. Psychopathological symptoms in adolescence	11
46. Pronounced traits of premorbid personality	23
47. Other psychopathological symptoms, syndromes and disorders in adult life	14
48. Continual psychic stress	49
49. Precipitating stress	56

Table A5. Reliability in terms of pairwise agreement a, π and φ for symptom items for which at least 20% but not more than 80% of the ratings were "present" (or "absent"). The coefficients for the same symptoms are also shown by centre

Symptomatic item	All centres			Basle			Montreal			Nagasaki			Teheran			Tokyo		
	a	π	φ	a	π	φ	a	π	φ	a	π	φ	a	π	φ	a	π	φ
3. Hoplessness	0.86	0.92	0.56	0.83	0.91	0.40	0.76	0.86	0.01	0.90	0.95	0.32	1.00	1.00	0.89	0.84	0.91	0.42
5. Tension	0.88	0.94	0.64	0.83	0.91	0.10	0.88	0.94	0.54	0.87	0.93	—	1.00	1.00	0.86	0.84	0.91	0.59
6. Aggression	0.88	0.93	0.73	0.83	0.91	0.49	0.96	0.98	0.84	1.00	1.00	0.94	1.00	1.00	0.80	0.70	0.82	0.38
9. Slowness of thought	0.88	0.94	0.70	0.75	0.85	0.30	0.80	0.89	0.51	1.00	1.00	—	0.95	0.97	0.88	0.82	0.90	0.46
10. Indecisiveness	0.91	0.96	0.77	0.67	0.79	0.10	0.92	0.96	0.77	1.00	1.00	0.82	1.00	1.00	0.66	0.89	0.94	0.68
13. Change of perception of time	0.92	0.96	0.79	0.92	0.96	0.66	0.96	0.98	0.80	1.00	1.00	0.88	1.00	1.00	0.88	0.82	0.90	0.56
14. Feelings of guilt	0.91	0.96	0.80	0.83	0.91	0.17	0.96	0.98	0.77	0.90	0.95	0.74	1.00	1.00	0.89	0.89	0.94	0.70
16. Hypochondriasis	0.86	0.92	0.63	0.92	0.96	0.52	0.84	0.91	0.15	0.74	0.85	0.41	1.00	1.00	0.84	0.89	0.94	0.64
17. Ideas of impoverishment	0.92	0.96	0.77	1.00	1.00	0.78	0.96	0.98	0.57	0.84	0.91	0.61	1.00	1.00	0.84	0.91	0.95	0.58
18. Suicidal ideas	0.92	0.96	0.81	0.92	0.96	0.52	1.00	1.00	0.90	1.00	1.00	0.90	1.00	1.00	0.89	0.80	0.88	0.55
19. Ideas of persecution	0.90	0.95	0.77	0.75	0.85	0.30	0.92	0.96	0.75	0.87	0.93	0.68	1.00	1.00	0.89	0.91	0.95	0.72
24. Psychomotor retardation	0.89	0.94	0.67	0.75	0.85	0.20	0.92	0.96	0.72	0.97	0.98	—	1.00	1.00	0.88	0.82	0.90	0.48
25. Psychomotor agitation	0.89	0.94	0.77	0.50	0.50	0.14	0.88	0.94	0.70	0.97	0.98	0.86	1.00	1.00	0.84	0.91	0.95	0.68
26. Lack of contact	0.85	0.92	0.63	0.92	0.96	0.27	0.88	0.94	0.66	0.84	0.91	0.06	0.95	0.97	0.56	0.77	0.87	0.50
27. Worse in morning	0.92	0.96	0.82	0.92	0.96	0.61	0.88	0.94	0.70	1.00	1.00	0.91	1.00	1.00	0.88	0.86	0.93	0.66
29. Decrease of libido	0.89	0.94	0.74	0.92	0.96	0.52	0.92	0.96	0.72	0.87	0.93	0.62	1.00	1.00	0.89	0.84	0.91	0.62
30. Early awakening	0.93	0.96	0.84	0.92	0.96	0.66	0.92	0.96	0.72	0.97	0.98	0.78	0.95	0.97	0.75	0.91	0.95	0.74
31. Inability to fall asleep	0.90	0.95	0.74	1.00	1.00	0.70	0.92	0.96	0.72	0.90	0.95	0.53	1.00	1.00	0.89	0.82	0.90	0.57
32. Fitful sleep	0.89	0.94	0.72	1.00	1.00	0.70	0.72	0.83	0.35	1.00	1.00	0.73	1.00	1.00	0.89	0.84	0.91	0.62
33. Lack of appetite	0.96	0.98	0.88	1.00	1.00	0.70	0.96	0.98	0.81	0.95	1.00	0.90	0.95	0.97	0.79	0.93	0.96	0.78
34. Change of weight	0.96	0.98	0.90	0.83	0.91	0.49	1.00	1.00	0.92	0.97	0.98	0.84	1.00	1.00	0.89	0.95	0.98	0.86
35. Constipation	0.92	0.96	0.83	0.75	0.85	—	0.96	0.98	0.84	0.97	0.98	0.86	0.95	0.97	0.79	0.91	0.95	0.78
36. Feelings of pressure	0.94	0.97	0.85	0.92	0.96	0.68	0.96	0.98	0.84	0.97	0.97	0.64	0.95	0.97	0.56	0.93	0.96	0.81
37. Other somatic signs	0.91	0.95	0.80	1.00	1.00	0.78	0.92	0.96	0.70	0.94	0.97	0.81	1.00	1.00	0.86	0.82	0.90	0.58
38. Other symptoms I	0.82	0.90	0.60	1.00	1.00	0.70	0.84	0.91	0.38	0.81	0.89	0.54	1.00	1.00	0.89	0.70	0.82	0.28
39. Other symptoms II	0.90	0.95	0.69	0.92	0.96	—	1.00	1.00	0.73	0.81	0.89	0.49	1.00	1.00	0.84	0.86	0.93	0.63

Table A6. Intercentre reliability exercise: Percentage positive ratings of symptoms and signs

Symptom	% rated present
1. Sadness	96
2. Joylessness, inability to enjoy	84
3. Hopelessness	75
4. Anxiety	79
5. Tension	64
6. Aggression, irritability	41
7. Lack of energy	93
8. Disruption of social functioning	89
9. Slowness and retardation of thought	80
10. Indecisiveness	72
11. Loss of interest	81
12. Loss of ability to concentrate	81
13. Change of perception of time	50
14. Feelings of guilt and self-reproach	59
15. Ideas of insufficiency, inadequacy and worthlessness, lack of self-confidence	70
16. Hypochondriasis	18
17. Ideas of impoverishment	9
18. Suicidal ideas	59
19. Ideas of persecution and self-reference	84
20. Delusions of guilt	0
21. Delusions of hypochondriasis	0
22. Delusions of impoverishment and nihilism	0
23. Other delusions	0
24. Psychomotor retardation	71
25. Psychomotor agitation	24
26. Lack of contact	74
27. Worse in the morning	52
28. Worse in the evening	23
29. Decrease of libido	79
30. Early awakening	40
31. Inability to fall asleep	49
32. Fitful, restless sleep	38
33. Lack of appetite	51
34. Change of body weight	44
35. Constipation	32
36. Feelings of pressure or pain	51
37. Other somatic signs and symptoms	35
38. Other symptoms	28
39. Other symptoms	10

Past history items

40. History of psychiatric disorder in relatives (affective)	38
41. History of psychiatric disorder in relatives (general)	15
42. Early separation	1
43. Stressful events in childhood	14
44. Psychopathological symptoms in childhood	18
45. Psychopathological symptoms in adolescence	9
46. Pronounced traits of premorbid personality	30
47. Other psychopathological symptoms, syndromes and disorders in adult life	21
48. Continual psychic stress	21
49. Precipitating stress	39

Table A7. Reliability in terms of π, φ and pairwise agreement ratio 'a' for symptom items for which not less than 20% and not more than 80% of the ratings (during the intercentre reliability exercises) were rated present (or absent)

Symptom item	a	π	φ
1. Sadness	0.95	0.97	0.27
2. Joylessness	0.82	0.90	0.14
7. Lack of energy	0.89	0.94	0.15
8. Disruption of social functioning	0.91	0.95	0.53
9. Slowness of thought	0.76	0.86	0.06
11. Loss of interest	0.87	0.93	0.53
12. Loss of ability to concentrate	0.73	0.84	0.07
16. Hypochondriasis	0.77	0.87	0.09
17. Ideas of impoverishment	0.87	0.93	0.03
19. Ideas of persecution and self-reference	0.84	0.91	0.54
20. Delusions of guilt	1.00	1.00	—
21. Delusions of hypochondriasis	1.00	1.00	—
22. Delusions of impoverishment	0.96	0.98	0.49
23. Other delusions	1.00	1.00	—
39. Other symptoms	0.89	0.94	0.21

Table A8. Comparison of π, φ and pairwise agreement ratio 'a' for intra- and intercentre reliability exercises. Only those symptoms are listed for which the frequency of the ratings for symptom presence and symptom absence ranged between 20% and 80%

Symptom item	Intracentre reliability			Intercentre reliability			Difference in terms of π
	a	π	φ	a	π	φ	π
6. Aggression	0.87	0.93	0.73	0.63	0.75	0.15	0.18
10. Indecisiveness	0.92	0.96	0.77	0.68	0.80	0.15	0.15
13. Change of perception of time	0.92	0.96	0.79	0.84	0.91	0.54	0.05
14. Feeling of guilt	0.92	0.96	0.80	0.77	0.87	0.45	0.09
18. Suicidal ideas	0.92	0.96	0.81	0.63	0.75	0.23	0.21
25. Psychomotor agitation	0.89	0.94	0.77	0.76	0.86	0.25	0.08
26. Lack of contact	0.85	0.92	0.63	0.77	0.87	0.27	0.05
27. Worse in the morning	0.92	0.96	0.82	0.61	0.73	0.13	0.23
29. Decrease of libido	0.89	0.94	0.74	0.79	0.88	0.32	0.06
30. Early awakening	0.92	0.96	0.84	0.68	0.80	0.19	0.15
31. Inability to fall asleep	0.91	0.95	0.74	0.76	0.86	0.38	0.09
32. Fitful, restless sleep	0.89	0.94	0.72	0.67	0.79	0.14	0.15
33. Lack of appetite	0.96	0.98	0.88	0.87	0.93	0.72	0.05
34. Change of body weight	0.96	0.98	0.90	0.68	0.80	0.34	0.17
35. Constipation	0.92	0.96	0.83	0.89	0.94	0.72	0.02
36. Feelings of pressure	0.94	0.97	0.85	0.85	0.92	0.65	0.05
37. Other somatic signs	0.91	0.95	0.80	0.77	0.87	0.38	0.08
Arithmetic mean	0.91	0.95	0.79	0.74	0.84	0.37	0.11
Standard deviation	0.03	0.02	0.07	0.09	0.07	0.21	0.06

Table A9. Reliability in terms of π for past history items for which not more than 20% of the ratings were scored present

Past history items	π
41. History of psychiatric disorder in relatives (general)	0.90
42. Early separation	0.99
43. Stressful events in childhood	0.93
44. Psychopathological symptoms in childhood	0.92
45. Psychopathological symptoms in adolescence	0.93

Annex 2

Screening form

Patient's surname (optional) _____

Patient's first name _____

Age _____   Sex _____
      (in years)

EXCLUSION CATEGORIES
(ring)

1. Definite physical disease, toxic disorder or cerebral damage or disease
2. Mental retardation (IQ 70 or less)
3. Presence of one or more of the following symptoms:
    - 3.1. Thought withdrawal or intrusion, echo of thoughts
    - 3.2. Delusion of being controlled
    - 3.3. Elaborate delusional system of delusions other than guilt, hypochondriasis, impoverishment, nihilism
    - 3.4. Elaborate hallucinations with content other than depressive (e.g., not a voice calling the patient names, or saying "kill yourself" etc.)
4. Presence of severe language or hearing difficulties

INCLUSION CATEGORIES

Presence of at least two of the following symptoms:
(ring as many as present)

1. Depressive mood
2. Suicidal thoughts
3. Hopelessness
4. Feeling of worthlessness
5. Hypochondriasis and/or anxiety
6. Feeling of diminution of ability
7. Self-reproach or guilt
8. Inability to feel or enjoy

This patient is (ring):

      Excluded

      Included
      if included
      WHO number _____

WHO/MH 5185 12/72-1000

Annex 3

WHO Schedule for a Standardized Assessment of Depressive Disorders (WHO/SADD) — 5th Revision

Name of facility in which the patient is treated

....

Patient's reference number in facility in which he is treated

....

Patient's first name

....

Optional

Patient's surname

....

Patient's permanent address

....

....

Any other address through which patient could be traced

....

....

Informant's name and address

....

....

Name of psychiatrist in charge of patient in facility

....

Introductory note

This schedule is composed of three parts: part one covers basic data necessary for the identification of the patient; part two a series of rating scales for the assessment of the clinical condition of the patient and items to cover the psychiatric history; and the third part covers the diagnosis and the classification of the diagnosis.

The rater should enter the code number of the answer into the boxes provided. In all instances the entries should be the best estimate that examining psychiatrists can make using all available information. Thus in the clinical part, for example, the rating should be made taking into account: the interview, the ward behaviour report, case notes, information from relatives and other informants, etc.

PART 1. IDENTIFICATION DATA   Study No. | R 6 2 |

Card 1
cols.
1–3

1.1 Centre at which the interview was conducted   4–5
    21 = Basle
    22 = Montreal
    23 = Nagasaki
    24 = Teheran
    25 = Tokyo

1.2 Patient's study number (three digits)   6–8

1.3 Was this schedule filled out as part of a reliability interview?   9
    0 = No
    1 = Yes, the psychiatrist who filled in this schedule also
        interviewed the patient
    2 = Yes, the psychiatrist who filled in this schedule was
        present during the interview but did *not* interview
        the patient himself

1.4 Psychiatrist who *filled in* this schedule   10–12

    Name ....   (Leave blank, will be
        coded centrally)

1.5 Psychiatrist who *interviewed* this patient   13–15

    Name ....   (Leave blank, will be
        coded centrally)

1.6 Age in years   16–17
    (Estimate if necessary)

1.7 Date of birth   1   18–24
    (Fill in 9s if unknown)   Day   Month   Year

1.8 Sex 1 = Male   25
        4 = Female

1.9 Date of interview   26–31
        Day   Month   Year

1.10 Residence
    1 = Urban
    2 = Rural
    3 = No permanent residence but lives in study area

    32

1.11 Patient's status
    1 = Inpatient
    2 = Outpatient
    3 = Day patient
    4 = Night patient
    5 = Other
    If "other" specify ....

    33

1.12 Marital status
    Rate for most of the time in last six months:
    1 = Single   5 = Widowed
    2 = Married   6 = Common law marriage
    3 = Divorced 9 = Not known
    4 = Separated

    34

1.13 How many hours did the patient work in his/her job?
    (Housewives' and students' working hours should also
    be estimated)
    1 = Worked 35 hours or more a week
    2 = Worked 10–34 hours a week
    3 = Worked less than 10 hours a week
    4 = Did not work
    9 = Unknown

    35

1.14 Highest level of education reached
    1 = Illiterate, no school
    2 = Less than 5 completed years of school
    3 = 5–12 completed years of school
    4 = More than 12 completed years of school but no
        completed university education
    5 = University graduate
    6 = Postgraduate education completed
    9 = Unknown

    36

1.15 Give description of what patient's occupation is:
    (Give details of what he/she actually does)

    (Leave blank)   37–40

    ....

    ....

    ....

    ....

1.16 Religion into which patient was born

    (Leave blank, will be
    coded centrally)   41–42

    ....
         (Specify)

1.17 Current religion

(Leave blank, will be
coded centrally)

....
(Specify)

1.18 How active do you consider the patient to be in his/her
religion (in comparison to others in the same social
and educational group)
0 = Not at all
1 = Less than average
2 = Average
3 = More than average
9 = Not known

45

1.19 Socioeconomic status in psychiatrist's judgement

46

    1   2   3   4   5   9

Highest   Lowest   Impossible
in the   in the   to estimate
culture   culture

1.20 Sources of information used in the assessment of this
patient (0 = No, 1 = Yes, 9 = Unknown)

  1.20.1 Interview with patient   47

  1.20.2 Observation of patient in the ward   48

  1.20.3 Case notes of previous admissions   49

  1.20.4 Case notes of present admission   50

  1.20.5 Information from interview with relatives   51

  1.20.6 Information from interview with other informants, e.g., patient's doctor, police   52

  1.20.7 Information from other written sources, e.g.,
court record, school record, etc.   53

  1.20.8 Other sources   54

....
(Specify)

PART 2. SYMPTOMS, SIGNS AND HISTORY

2.A Symptoms and signs

Coding instructions: 0 = Absent
1 = Present, mild
2 = Present, continuously or in severe form
9 = Interviewer not sure or information not sufficient

If no positive rating in rubric "last month", consider also rubric "any time in this episode". If rated positively under "last month" leave box "any time in this episode" empty.

Symptom number	Last month	Any time in this episode	Card 1 cols.
1. Sadness, depressed mood	☐	☐	55–56
2. Joylessness, inability to enjoy	☐	☐	57–58
3. Hopelessness	☐	☐	59–60
4. Anxiety and/or tension	☐	☐	61–62
5. Aggression	☐	☐	63–64
6. Irritability	☐	☐	65–66
7. Lack of energy	☐	☐	67–68
8. Disruption of social functioning	☐	☐	69–70
9. Desire to be alone	☐	☐	71–72
10. Subjective experience of slowness and retardation of thought (Rate 9 if question not understood by patient; objectively observed slowness should be rated in item 36.)	☐	☐	73–74
11. Indecisiveness	☐	☐	75–76
12. Lack of self-confidence	☐	☐	77–78
		1	80

			Card 2 cols.
13. Loss of interest	☐	☐	10–11
14. Loss of ability to concentrate	☐	☐	12–13
15. Subjective experience of loss of memory	☐	☐	14–15
16. Early awakening	☐	☐	16–17
17. Inability to fall asleep	☐	☐	18–19
18. Fitful, restless sleep	☐	☐	20–21
19. Hypersomnia	☐	☐	22–23

Card 2
cols.

20. Lack of appetite — 24–25

21. Change of body weight — 26–27

22. Constipation — 28–29

23. Feelings of pressure — 30–31

24. Other somatic signs and symptoms (specify) — 32–33

....

....

....

25. Other psychological symptoms (specify) — 34–35

....

....

....

26. Decrease of libido — 36–37

27. Change of perception of time — 38–39
    (If patient unable to understand question rate 9)

28. Suicidal ideas — 40–41

For the symptoms number 29–33 an additional code = 3 is to be used when the respective symptom is of delusional nature.

29. Feelings and/or ideas of guilt and self-reproach — 42–43

30. Ideas of insufficiency, inadequacy and worthlessness — 44–45

31. Hypochondriasis — 46–47

32. Ideas of impoverishment — 48–49

33. Ideas of reference and/or persecution — 50–51

34. Other delusions (specify) — 52–53

....

....

....

....

....

35. Disorders of perception: illusions or hallucinations ☐ ☐   54–55
    (Use code = 3 if hallucinations)

....

....

....

....

....

36. Psychomotor retardation   ☐ ☐   56–57

37. Psychomotor restlessness and agitation, diurnal ☐ ☐   58–59
    fluctuation of mood:

38. Worse in the morning than at any other time during ☐ ☐ 60–61
    the day

39. Worse in the evening than at any other time during ☐ ☐ 62–63
    the day

40. Physical disease or infirmity (specify)   ☐ ☐   64–65

....

....

....

2.B Psychiatric history

Coding instructions: 0 = Absent
                       1 = Present
                       2 = (For items 49 and 50 only) If particularly severe
                       9 = Interviewer not sure or information not sufficient

   For items 51 and 53 write number of episodes—e.g., 01 for one episode and 12 for twelve episodes. If unknown write 99. If no previous episode rate 00.
   For items 52 and 54 rate number of years from 01 (one year or less). If unknown write 99 and if no previous episodes write 00.

41. History of psychiatric disorder (affective) in blood relatives ☐   66

42. History of psychiatric disorder (other) in blood relatives   ☐   67

43. Early separation   ☐   68

Card 2
cols.

44. Stressful events in childhood (specify)   □   69

....

....

....

45. Psychopathological symptoms in childhood   □   70

46. Psychopathological symptoms in adolescence   □   71

47. Psychopathological symptoms, syndromes and disorders in   □   72
    adult life other than past or present affective disturbances

48. Pronounced traits of premorbid personality   □   73

49. Continual psychic stress (specify)   □   74

....

....

....

50. Precipitating stress (specify)   □   75

....

....

....

51. Number of previous depressive episodes   ⊞⊞   76–77

52. Number of years since first depressive episode   78–79

2   80

Card 3
cols.

53. Number of previous manic episodes   ⊞⊞   10–11

54. Number of years since first manic episode   12–13

55. Number of intervals free of symptoms   14–15

56. Type of onset of current episode   □   16
    1 = Clearly sudden (less than a week)
    2 = Slow, insidious
    9 = Unknown

Card 3
cols.

57. Duration of present condition
    0 = Less than 1 week
    1 = 1 week to less than 1 month
    2 = 1 month to less than 3 months
    3 = 3 months to less than 6 months
    4 = 6 months to less than 1 year
    5 = 1 year to less than 2 years
    6 = 2 years or more
    9 = Unknown

17

PART 3. TREATMENT IN PRESENT EPISODE

Coding instructions: 0 = No
1 = Yes
9 = Unknown

If rated positively under "last two weeks" leave box "any time in this episode" empty.

	Last two weeks	Any time in this episode	
3.1. Antidepressants (specify drug)	☐	☐	18–19
....			
3.2 Electroconvulsive treatment. Write number of treatments given. Under "any time in this episode" enter number of weeks (99 = unknown)	☐☐	☐☐	20–23
3.3 Lithium	☐	☐	24–25
3.4 MAO-Inhibitors	☐	☐	26–27
3.5 Major tranquillizers (neuroleptics)	☐	☐	28–29
(Specify drug)			
....			
3.6 Minor tranquillizers or anxiolytics	☐	☐	30–31
(Specify drug)			
....			
3.7 Sleep deprivation	☐	☐	32–33
3.8 Psychotherapy (specify method)	☐	☐	34–35
....			

* Rate 2, if serum lithium level during the last 6 months was permanently 0.6 mmol/l or higher.

Card 3
cols.

3.9 Other (specify)   □   □   36–37

....

....

PART 4. DIAGNOSIS AND CLASSIFICATION

4.1 Psychiatrist's clinical assessment of the overall
severity of the condition   □   38
1 = Mild
2 = Moderate
3 = Severe
4 = Very severe

4.2 State diagnosis, according to your own practice   □□□□   39–42
(Leave blank)

....

....

....

....

4.3 How would you classify your diagnosis according
to the ninth revision of the international
classification of diseases (ICD)? (Use as many
codes as necessary; start with the most
important diagnosis.) Write ICD code number in
the boxes—e.g. reactive depressive psychosis
298.0 =

1. □□□□   43–46

2. □□□□   47–50

□□□□   51–54

4. □□□□   55–58

| 2 | 9 | 8 | 0 |

5. □□□□   59–62

For convenience a list of the ICD-9 codes
for depressive conditions is given below:
295.7 Schizoaffective subtype of schizophrenia
296.1 Manic-depressive psychosis, depressed
type (monopolar depression)
296.3 Manic-depressive psychosis, circular (bipolar) type, currently depressed
296.4 Manic-depressive psychosis, circular (bipolar) type, mixed
296.6 Manic-depressive psychosis, other than unspecified
296.8 Other affective psychosis
296.9 Unspecified affective psychosis
298.0 Reactive (psychogenic) depressive psychosis
300.4 Neurotic depression
301.1 Depressive or cyclothymic personality
308.0 Acute reaction to stress with predominant
disturbance of emotions (depressive)

309.0 Brief depressive adjustment reaction
309.1 Prolonged depressive adjustment reaction
311   Depressive disorder, not elsewhere clas-
      sified

4.4 Information which could not be coded but which
you consider important in this case:

....

....

....

....

....

                                                    63–79
                        Leave blank

                                          3   80

Companion glossary for the WHO Schedule for a Standardized Assessment of Depressive Disorders (WHO/SADD) — 5th Revision

PART 1. IDENTIFICATION DATA

Items 1.1–1.9 inclusive, 1.11–1.17 inclusive, and 1.20 are self-explanatory. The definition of items 1.10, 1.18, and 1.19 may vary from culture to culture, and possibly within cultures as well. The investigators should develop a definition suitable for local conditions and test its applicability before embarking on investigations. The definition should contain elements such as name of district (in item 1.10) or indication of income available to patient and his household (item 1.19).

PART 2. SYMPTOMS, SIGNS AND HISTORY

General Considerations

1. The recommended probes and examples of responses given below for most of the items do not aim to exhaust the entire range of questions and answers possible in different settings.

2. Ratings should be based on clinical judgement or the best possible estimate taking into account all the sources of information available: interview with the patient, the ward behaviour report, case notes, information from relatives and other informants, etc.

3. Patients may find the questions for certain items difficult to understand and answer. The investigators should use clinical skills and their knowledge of local conditions to ensure that the patient understands the questions. If the patients cannot describe symptoms clearly, rate 9.

Part 2A. Symptoms and signs

1. **Sadness, depressed mood.** Unpleasant affective state characterized by emotional dejection, feelings of sadness or misery. The symptom of sadness, or depressed mood, should not be rated as present if it is experienced only for a very short time, e.g., a few hours.

Recommended probes:

- How have you been feeling lately?
- Do you feel sad, downcast or miserable?
- Have you felt sad without really knowing why?
- Have you felt like crying, or as though everything around you was dark and black?

Examples of characteristic responses

Although responses may vary both between and within cultures, depressed patients usually describe their mood state in a fairly similar manner. Cultural variation can be found in the frequency with which metaphors or figurative language are used to convey depressive feelings—for example, the heart may be "heavy", "dark", "constricted", "sunk", or the patient may feel as if he had "a stone in the heart", or a "dark cloud over his head". Such metaphoric expressions appear to be more frequent in non-European cultures (e.g., Japan and Iran). In some cultures, particular aspects of the experience of being sad or depressed receive emphasis—e.g., feeling lonely or pitying oneself (Japan), feeling like crying (Canada), or no longer keen on anything (Switzerland).

2. **Joylessness, inability to enjoy.** Subjective experience of a loss of the ability to derive pleasure from ordinary activities and happenings of daily life, or to cherish things to which the patient had previously been emotionally attached.

Recommended probes:

- Can you enjoy doing anything?
- Is there anything that you like to look forward to?
- Have you noticed that recently you have not been able to enjoy anything, for instance a good dinner, a film, a trip, sex, or anything else that used to give you pleasure?
- Do you feel less cheerful and joyless, as if barren?
- Do you have the feeling that nothing in the world can excite you, that you are no longer able to laugh with your whole heart?

Examples of characteristic responses

Not all patients who have this symptom are clearly aware of it or describe it spontaneously. When asked, however, they readily recognize the experience of joylessness and inability to enjoy. This seems to be more often the case in cultures where there is less emphasis on leisure activities and less normative expectation of experiencing positive pleasure (e.g., in Japan). Nevertheless, when asked, patients in different cultures describe the symptom in terms of loss of sensitivity or eagerness ("don't care any more"—Switzerland; being unable to get "turned on"—Canada; loss of "heart" and inability to feel happy—Iran; inability to enjoy the company of others—Japan) and general diminution or loss of the capacity for pleasurable experiences (all centres).

3. **Hopelessness.** Lack of hope or of positive expectations about one's own future.

Recommended probes:

● How do you feel about the future?
● Do you have any hope that things will get better again?
● Do you see the gloomy side of life only, as far as you are concerned?

Examples of characteristic responses

Patients complain of having no hope in life, and no hope of getting well. Expressions like "I see only darkness in the future", "cannot see any way out", "I feel as if confronted by a wall", "there is no help or hope for me", "there is nothing to strive for", etc., appear to be common in different cultural settings.

4. **Anxiety and/or tension**

(a) **Anxiety.** Unpleasant emotional state characterized by fear without apparent reason or by intense worrying about things that might happen; its intensity may vary from a vague, uneasy feeling of fear to panic attacks; it is often accompanied by physiological signs, such as heart palpitations, sweaty hands, etc.

Recommended probes:

● Do you feel anxious, fearful or just uneasy without any clear reason?
● Do you get the feeling as if something horrible is going to happen?
● Do you feel as if trembling inside?

Examples of characteristic responses

There is considerable variation, both across and within cultures, in how anxiety is expressed. The word "anxiety" does not have clear equivalents in some languages although the subjective experience to which the term refers seems to be universal. Patients in some cultures (e.g., in Canada and Switzerland) may be more prone to describing the mental components of anxiety ("I feel anxious", "afraid for no reason", "afraid of everything") than patients in other cultures (e.g., Iran, Japan) where the physical sensations associated with anxiety are usually more stressed ("my heart is pounding", "can't get to sleep because I feel nervous inside", "pressure in my chest", etc). Some languages (e.g., Farsi) are very rich in expressions related to the various aspects of anxiety—"heart upset" is a common phrase describing anxiety and has a connotation very similar to that of the English phrase "butterflies in the stomach". Sometimes the description of anxiety is associated with the idea of some kind of action, like having the urge to run away from the room. A characteristic expression of anxiety feelings in Japan is the statement of the patient that he may "do" something terrible.

(*Note*: Panic attacks associated with phobic reactions are rated in Item 25.)

(b) **Tension.** Unpleasant emotional state characterized primarily by inability to relax, usually accompanied by increased muscular tone, and sometimes by physiological symptoms or signs—e.g., heart palpitations and galvanic skin response changes. This symptom is often difficult to separate clearly from anxiety, with which it often coexists. Tension may also be associated with a feeling of inner restlessness. It should be noted, however, that observable agitation is rated in Item 37.

Recommended probes:

● Do you feel tensed up, so that you cannot relax or keep still?
● Do you feel like pacing up and down?
● Do you feel that your muscles are tight?
● Do you feel at ease?

Examples of characteristic responses

Most patients describe tension as inability to relax; muscles (e.g., at the back of the neck, the forehead, or the forearms) feel tight; the patient must do something, e.g., take a drink or perform a physical exercise, to ease this unpleasant sensation. In some cultures (e.g., Japan) patients tend to describe feelings of tension as "nervousness". Since this expression also has the connotation of irritability, it may be necessary to use additional probes to obtain a clear description of the symptom.

5. **Aggression.** Acts of violence or destruction intended to damage or harm things, animals or people. If aggressive acts are directed towards inanimate objects, rate 1 or 2 depending on the frequency and severity of such behaviour. If aggression is discharged toward people or animals, rate always 2 and, whenever possible, supplement the rating with a brief narrative description of the aggressive act(s). Outbursts of verbal abuse should be rated in Item 6.

Recommended probes:

● Have you lost your temper at any time recently?
● To the extent that you would hit, or otherwise harm anyone, e.g., your spouse, child, or other people?
● Have you been violent to animals, for example pets?
● Have you lost your temper and smashed things or caused any other property damage?

Examples of characteristic responses

Patient broke, smashed or tore things, handled domestic animals violently, inflicted pain, hit or beat up people. Note that only *overt* behaviour *aimed* at harming people or animals or damaging objects should qualify as aggression. Non-deliberate or accidental damage should not be rated here, even if a depressed patient attaches particular importance to such occurrences.

6. **Irritability.** Lowered tolerance for daily events that did not usually irritate the patient before this episode started. Abnormal readiness to flare up in anger, whether shown or bottled up, and outbursts of verbal abuse, should be rated as a more severe degree of irritability.

Recommended probes:

● Do you get angry or irritable more easily than has been usual for you?
● Do you feel more touchy than usual?
● Do you fly off the handle more easily?
● Do you tend to spark off at the slightest annoyance?
● Do you use coarse language when you feel irritated?

Examples of characteristic responses

Patients describe themselves as quarrelsome, disturbed by trifles, annoyed more easily than usual, being no longer able to put up with anything, or as "nervous" (probe further to distinguish from tension—Item 4(b). The acceptability of manifestations of irritability varies across cultures. Irritability is, for example, less acceptable in Japan than in some other cultures. Some cross-cultural differences must be borne in mind and the threshold for a positive rating of the symptom adjusted accordingly, if comparable assessments are to be obtained from different cultural settings.

7. **Lack of energy.** The patient complains or his intimates observe that he becomes tired more easily and that doing trivial things has become more difficult; the symptom includes any degree of diminution of energy from difficulty in performing daily tasks to feeling tired all day, and being unable to work at all.

Recommended probes:

● Do you have as much energy as usual?
● Can you do as much as you used to?
● Has your strength decreased?
● Do you get tired more easily and have to give up?
● Do you feel that getting up in the morning and starting the day is more difficult than it used to be?

Examples of characteristic responses

The patient feels listless, or tired all the time, has no energy at all, is unable to work, complains that "moving about is difficult". Sometimes lack of energy is described as "feeling dull" or "sleepy" all day long. There appears to be little cultural variation in the manifestation of this symptom.

8. **Disruption of social functioning.** Impaired performance of social roles and non-response to social obligations since the appearance of symptoms. The presence of a disruption of social functioning should be considered in terms of: (*a*) relationships within the family; (*b*) social relationships outside the family (e.g., workmates, neighbours, friends, participation in community affairs or other group activities); (*c*) ability to perform work routines (where relevant). With regard to (*a*) and (*b*), disruption of social functioning should be rated as present either when the social interaction of the patient is characterized by friction, conflicts, excessive dependency, etc., or when the patient withdraws from social contacts. With regard to (*c*), disruption of social functioning should be rated as present if the quantity or quality of the patient's output at work has deteriorated from his previous standards, or if he can no longer conform to the daily routine of work. Rate 1 if a marked disturbance is described in any *one* area: (*a*), (*b*), or (*c*). If more than one area is affected, rate 2. If the patient is admitted to hospital during this episode, rate 2.

Recommended probes:

- How have you been getting along with your spouse, parents, children?
- Do you feel irritable with them?
- Or do you feel that you have lost interest in them, to the extent of talking with them less than before?
- Have you wished to stay away from people, even from those who are closest to you?
- How have you been getting along with your friends, or neighbours, lately?
- Do you find that you see them now less often than before or that you get impatient in their presence?
- How about social (sports, religion, etc.) activities?
- Do you participate in group activities less than you used to?
- Do you find that going to work is an intolerable burden for you?
- Do you feel you are as productve as before?

Examples of characteristic responses

The patient describes constant quarrelling with spouse; may be considering divorce; feels no longer able to tolerate the presence of other people, even closest relatives and members of his family; or tends to stay alone and "wishes to be left in peace". Clubs, sports, community or church affairs, or any other social gatherings attract him no longer. Work has deteriorated and is experienced as a burden impossible to carry. The culturally specific forms of a disruption of social functioning due to a depressive illness may vary but the three areas in which such impairments occur: family, social group, and work, can be identified and explored in a similar fashion in most settings.

9. **Desire to be alone.** Patient states that he wishes to be alone because of a feeling of isolation from other people and inability to communicate with them. Communication with people is experienced as a burden or a strain.

(*Note.* If the patient withdraws from other people or isolates himself, rate both Items 8 and 9 as present. If the patient says he cannot communicate with others but still attends social events rate this item 1 or 2; Item 8 would then be rated 0 or 1, depending on the presence/absence of disturbances described under 8(c).)

Recommended probes:

- Do you want to be alone?
- Do you want to stay away from people?
- Do you find talking or listening to people a great strain?
- Are you more comfortable when you are alone than when you are with other people?

Examples of characteristic responses

The patient has fewer contacts with other people, feels shy and withdrawn in their presence, would rather withdraw into his own shell, would like to "get away from it all", or "go to some quiet place alone". The presenting characteristics of this symptom appear to be similar in various cultural settings.

10. **Subjective experience of slowness and retardation of thought.** Patient feels that his thinking is slowed down, muddled, or inefficient. It is important to note that the rating of this symptom should be based on the description of the patient's *subjective* experience, not his observed speed of response during the interview, which is rated in Item 36. The symptom "subjective feeling that one's movements are slowed down" should be rated in Item 25.

Recommended probes:

- Can you think as quickly and clearly as before?
- Do you feel that your thinking is slowed down, or your thoughts get muddled up?

Examples of characteristic responses

Thoughts come more slowly, ideas do not come as easily, thinking straight requires great effort. It should be noted that the reported, subjectively experienced retardation of thought may not correspond to the patient's rate and speed of verbal response during the interview.

11. **Indecisiveness.** Difficulty and marked hesitation in choosing between alternatives when doing trivial or routine tasks. Decisions are reached with considerable delay. Anxiety usually occurs when a decision is required; the patient may regret and ruminate over decisions made. The item should not be rated as present if in the opinion of the interviewer the decision required is difficult for the average person.

Recommended probes:

- Do you find it hard to make decisions?
- Can you make decisions about ordinary things—choosing what clothes to put on or what food to buy—as easily as you used to?
- Are you often "in two minds", even if quite ordinary decisions have to be made?

Examples of characteristic responses

The patient complains that he finds it more difficult than usual to make up his mind, that he feels very anxious when he has to make a decision, or regrets the decision made. Idioms like "being in two minds" (Japan) or "being two-hearted" (Iran) may be used by patients to describe the same basic experience.

12. **Lack of self-confidence.** Experience of lacking confidence in one's ability to communicate and interact with people, to perform well at work, and with one's family; a feeling of inadequacy in most activities involving interaction with other people.

Recommended probes:

● Do you feel self-confident enough when dealing with other people?
● Do you anticipate discomfort or failure, or both, when communicating with people, for example, when working at your job, or when with your family?
● Do you feel that you are easily manipulated by other people?

Examples of characteristic responses

The patient feels inadequate in his daily duties, including his job or his family; feels that he is not a strong personality, or that he is easily put upon by others.

13. **Loss of interest.** The appeal of daily tasks and social life is absent. The patient does not want to take part in any kind of activities because they do not attract him. This item should be rated as 'present' even if the patient still partakes in an activity but has lost all interest in it. It may be difficult to distinguish loss of interest from lack of interest existing before the present illness and from joylessness. The former should be distinguished by inquiry about the time when the symptom occurred. Lack of interest should not be rated positive in the instance of joylessness. It is likely that extreme joylessness will always be accompanied by loss of interest; the opposite is not necessarily the case since it may happen that the patient, though having lost interest in most things, retains some interests and enjoys engaging in some activities. It is important to recall that the amount of interest a person has normally varies greatly from individual to individual.

Recommended probes:

● Have you lost interest in things that used to interest you?
● Do you find that you do not care about anything any more, or at least not as much as you used to?
● Have you got the same interest as always in your family? (Inquiries about "interest in housework" among women, and about "interest in work and/or hobbies" are the most common examples used in all cultures.)

Examples of characteristic responses

The patient describes loss of interest in one or more activities, such as work, housework, hobbies, reading, newspapers, pets, watching television. The inquiry about loss of interest appears to elicit similar responses from depressed patients in different cultures.

14. **Loss of ability to concentrate.** Difficulty in focusing and sustaining attention. The interviewer's probing about this item should proceed so as to distinguish loss of the ability to concentrate from "Subjective experience of slowness and retardation of thought" (Item 10) and "Subjective experience of loss of memory" (Item 15). Do not rate positive if the patient stopped engaging in an activity because of loss of interest (e.g., not following a TV programme through).

Recommended probes:

● Can you concentrate on what you are doing as well as before?
● Can you concentrate on your daily tasks and activities?
● Is it more difficult for you to read a book or even a newspaper?
● Can you follow right through a television programme, or do you lose the thread of the action?
● Have you become more forgetful lately?

Examples of characteristic responses

Difficulty in collecting thoughts, "cannot concentrate on my newspaper", "cannot concentrate on what people are saying", "cannot concentrate on my favourite television programme". The patient may describe a feeling of "heaviness in the head", or of being unable to "think a matter through", and tends to avoid thinking about complicated matters.

15. **Subjective experience of loss of memory.** The patient feels that his memory is failing him, that his ability to recollect important facts and events is decreasing. The rating of this item should be based on the patient's reported subjective experience, without considering his objective level of performance on memory tasks or tests.

Recommended probes:

● Is your memory now as sharp as before?
● Do you feel that you are more forgetful now?
● Can you remember names, places, and important events as clearly as before?

Examples of characteristic responses

The patient feels he is absent-minded, that he mislays things more often, or describes worrying about what he feels is a deterioration of his memory.

16. **Early awakening.** Awakening at least 2 hours earlier than usual and inability to fall asleep again.

Recommended probes:

● Do you wake up earlier than usual in the morning?
● How much earlier?
● If you do not take any sleeping pills, would you wake up earlier than is normal for you?

Examples of characteristic responses

The patient describes a pattern of early awakening, usually 2–3 hours before the habitual time, and inability to go back to sleep. The question "Do you wake up early?" may be misunderstood in some cultures. For example, *zood*, the Farsi word for "early", has also the meaning of "rapidly". Additional probe-questions should be asked in such instances, and the investigator should make sure that the patient understands the intended meaning of the questions.

17. **Inability to fall asleep.** Inability to fall asleep within 2 hours of wanting to do so. If the patient takes sleeping pills prescribed specifically for this complaint, the symptom should always be rated as present, regardless of the duration of delays in falling asleep.

Recommended probes:

● Do you have difficulty falling asleep, even when you want to do so?
● Do you deliberately delay going to bed for fear of not being able to fall asleep?
● Do you need a sleeping pill to fall asleep?

Examples of characteristic responses

The patient complains of trouble falling asleep, lies awake for a long time, or delays going to bed for fear of not being able to fall asleep.

18. **Fitful, restless sleep.** Sleep is interrupted several times during the night for no apparent reason. Usually, the patient feels tired and not rested enough in the morning. The symptom should be rated as present if the patient takes sleeping pills and says that his sleep would be fitful without the medication.

Recommended probes:

● Do you tend to wake up more than once during the night?
● Do you feel fresh and well rested in the morning?
● Do you sleep through the night?
● Is your sleep fitful or restless?
● Do you feel as if you had not slept at all?

Examples of characteristic responses

Patient wakes up several times in the night, keeps waking up during the night, feels tired in the morning.

19. **Hypersomnia.** Total sleeping time during the day or night is increased by at least 2 hours, compared to the patient's habitual pattern. The symptom should be rated as present only if hypersomnia has been continuous for at least one week.

Recommended probes:

● Do you sleep more than was usual for you each day?
● Do you tend to fall asleep for brief spells during the day?

Examples of characteristic responses

The patient awakes 2 or more hours later than usual, complains of always being sleepy, even during the day; sleep is much longer than usual.

20. **Lack of appetite.** Diminished interest in or desire for food; eating is experienced as an effort. It should be emphasized that the quantity of food eaten may or may not be diminished.

Recommended probes:

● Has your appetite or taste for food changed?
● Do you have to force yourself to take food?
● Do you enjoy your meals?

Examples of characteristic responses

The patient has lost his taste for food, has to force himself to eat, has no appetite, does not enjoy meals.

21. **Change of body weight.** Loss (or gain) of weight beyond the patient's usual weight range. Clearly described loss (or gain) of weight during the current episode qualifies for a positive rating, even if weight has returned to normal (e.g., as result of treatment). To assess this symptom the rater should try to ascertain the weight pattern of the patient before illness. The sign "change of body weight" should be rated as present also if the patient has lost weight earlier during this episode and gained subsequently, e.g., because of successful treatment.

Recommended probes:

● Have you lost or gained weight during the last month, or since you first noticed a change in mood?
● If so, how much?
● How much did you weigh before?
● How much do you weigh now?

Examples of characteristic responses

Clothes do not fit as well any more, patient knows he has lost/gained weight.

22. **Constipation.** A condition in which the bowels are evacuated at longer intervals and with greater difficulty than usual.

Recommended probes:

● Are you constipated?
● Do your bowels move as often as usual?
● Do you have to take laxatives?

Examples of characteristic responses

The patient has bowel movements less often than usual, feels that a greater physical effort than usual is required to move bowels; laxatives are used now.

23. **Feelings of pressure.** Sensations of pressure in parts of the body, often changing from day to day. Description of this symptom is usually not precise and further probes are necessary.

Recommended probes:

● Do you now—unlike when you still felt well—experience a peculiar sensation of pressure in the chest, in the head, or anywhere else in your body?
● A sensation you did not have before?
● Have you developed uncomfortable sensations in any part of your body?

Examples of characteristic responses

Feels as if chest, stomach, or head is clamped in a vice.

24. **Other somatic signs and symptoms.** Complaints about dysfunction of various body organs, or of pains or aches not mentioned previously; presumed side-effects of psychotropic drugs are also rated here. Each sign and symptom should be described briefly.

Recommended probe:

● Do you have any other physical symptoms, aches, or pains, that I did not ask you about previously?

Examples of characteristic responses

A variety of complaints: aches or pains in head, chest, limbs, back or stomach; loss of hair; dry mouth; difficulty in passing urine; cold hands and feet; dry skin; chills in the limbs; blurred vision; buzzing sensation in the ears; skin eruption; vaginal discharge; menstrual periods shorter, delayed, or absent; dizziness, palpitations (if not rated in Item 4). Disturbances of sexual potency should be rated under Item 26. It should be noted that some of the complaints described by patients in response to the questions above may be related to side-effects of medication. Suspicion of this, however, should not discount them. In such cases the interviewer is requested to make a narrative note in the schedule. Rate positive also if symptom's existence began before present illness.

25. **Other psychological symptoms.** Any psychological symptoms not mentioned previously are rated here. Each symptom described by the patient

should be recorded in a brief narrative note. This item can be conveniently rated at the end of the interview.

Recommended probes:

● Are you aware of any other symptoms or changes that I have not asked you about?
● For example, do you have to repeat some act again and again that you cannot resist repeating, e.g., rechecking things, washing your hands?
● Do you feel that there is any kind of interference with your thoughts?
● Any other unusual experiences?
● Do you ever seem to hear noises or voices when there is no one about, and nothing else to explain it? (If evidence of hallucinations, make a rating in Item 35.)

Examples of characteristic responses

Obsessional ideas, compulsive acts and rituals are frequently described by patients in response to specific probing. Depersonalization, derealization, homicidal thoughts, nightmares, increased appetite, increased libido or panic attacks associated with phobic reactions may also be described. The interviewer should not fail to probe for psychotic symptoms, like hallucinations or subjective thought disorder, even if there is little on the surface to suggest their presence. This can best be done in examining patients' responses to Items 32–34.

26. **Decrease of libido.** Decrease of sexual performance or satisfaction; lesser reply to previously erotically stimulating situations. Do not rate positive if patient complains that he is not interested in sex any more but sexual functions are maintained. In such instances rate Item 13 positive.

Recommended probes:

Cultural norm and convention should be an important consideration in choosing the questions to be asked. Some questions of fairly wide acceptability in different cultures are:

● Have you lost interest in sex?
● Has your desire for sexual activity diminished? In what way?
● Is your sexual life the way it used to be? If changed, how?
● How is your marital life?
● Do you find it difficult or impossible to have sex?

It should be remembered that in some cultures (e.g., Islamic) most women feel uneasy speaking about their sexual life to the doctor. They seldom complain about lack of interest in sexual activity although they would answer affirmatively when asked. In such settings married women may be asked casually "How do you get on with your husband?" "Is there harmony between you and your husband?" The interviewer then proceeds, asking "Do you feel any desire for your husband?" or "How is your sexual life?" The situation is more difficult with widows and young girls. In most cases, one limits oneself to asking "Have you noticed any change in your feelings towards your fiancé or your boy-friend?" If the interviewer doubts whether the questions were understood, or whether the answers are candid, a rating of 9 is given. Men, in most cultures, contrary to women, describe their sexual lives frankly, often reporting impotence as a chief complaint.

Examples of characteristic responses

The patient no longer has any sexual needs, very little sexual desire left, does not enjoy sexual activity any more, gets no satisfaction from it, cannot perform the sexual act.

27. Change of perception of time. Subjective experience that time is passing in an unusual way: either too slowly, or too fast.

Recommended probe:

● Have you been aware of any changes in the way time has been passing for you, for example, moving more slowly than usual, or faster than usual?

The interviewer should satisfy himself that the patient understands the meaning of the question.

Examples of characteristic responses

The patient describes a feeling that time is dragging on, or speeding by; that an hour lasts as long as a year, or a minute; that time is standing still. If in spite of probing and cross-examining, the interviewer is not certain that the patient has understood the question, a rating of 9 should be made.

28. Suicidal ideas. Thoughts that life is not worth living; the patient may express the wish that he were dead, or describe an intention to put an end to his own life. It is important to be aware that suicidal ideas or intentions may be expressed directly or indirectly. A rating of 2 should always be made if suicidal attempts have taken place during this episode, when suicidal ideas are pronounced, or when specific plans for suicide have been made.

Recommended probes:

Direct questioning about suicidal ideas is always recommended and, contrary to some beliefs, generally it does not seem to upset depressive patients unduly.

Examples of such questions are:

● Do you ever wish you were dead?
● Do you find life not worth living?
● Do you find your life useless or empty?
● Do you ever think about suicide, or feel an urge to end it all?
● Have you made specific plans?
● How would you do it?
● Have you attempted suicide in the past?

Following the questions about presence of suicidal ideas, the investigator should also explore whether the patient has scruples against performing a suicidal act (e.g., concern for family, religious or ethical scruples, etc.).

Examples of characteristic responses

Life appears meaningless, patient wishes he were not alive or that something would happen to him, has suicidal thoughts, has written a letter admitting plans, has specific ideas how he will commit suicide (and may already have made at least one suicide attempt in the current episode).

29. **Feelings and/or ideas of guilt and self-reproach.** Painful awareness of having committed offences against one's moral code, or having failed to perform a duty or a task.

(*Note.* A rating of 3, delusional ideas of guilt, should be made if the patient describes an unshakeable belief in his own guilt, in having committed a crime, etc. Such beliefs cannot be reversed by evidence to the contrary and are out of keeping with the patient's social and cultural background—i.e., are not mere exaggerations of feelings that would be normal under the circumstances.)

Recommended probes:

● Do you feel guilty or reproach yourself about anything in particular you are doing now, or have done in your past: anything involving your family, friends, employers, or people in general, for example?
● Do you feel that you are a sinner or that you have committed a crime or an offence?
● Do you feel that you have not fulfilled your (religious, social, family) duties well?

Examples of characteristic responses

Nondelusional responses may include feelings of regret for something the patient has done, or has failed to do; that he has done something harmful to other people; that he has made many mistakes or "done everything wrong"; that he is sinful; he reproaches himself for a minor omission. Delusional responses may include the firm conviction that the patient is the worst possible person or the greatest criminal or sinner, has ruined his own life and that of others, has committed unpardonable crimes, is damned forever, or is responsible for all the misery in the world. The expression of guilt feelings and ideas varies considerably among cultures and individuals. In some instances, the patient describes in great detail his presumed offences and sins and insists on being punished. In other instances, the patient may wish to conceal his guilt feelings because of fear of retribution or punishment if they were revealed.

30. **Ideas of insufficiency, inadequacy, and worthlessness.** Feelings of inadequacy at work, or in performing obligations toward his family, or in other social relationships. Patient may feel worthless, or a burden to others. A rating of 3, delusional intensity of the symptoms, should be made if the patient's belief that he is worthless or a burden to others cannot be reversed by evidence to the contrary, and is out of keeping with his social and cultural background. Do not

rate positive if patient's answer indicates a realistic assessment of the situation, e.g., that he is a burden to others, having lost his job/income or because of disease.

Recommended probes:

- Have you lost some of your self-confidence?
- Do you feel worthless, that you are good for nothing?
- Have you lost your self-respect?
- Do you think that you are no longer of any use to anyone at your work, in your family, or in your circle of friends?
- Do you feel a burden to others?
- Do you think you are no longer able to achieve anything?

Examples of characteristic responses

Among nondelusional responses may be the feeling that the patient has no personal worth, that he may be a burden to others; that he cannot do his job well; feels inadequate; feels he is not fulfilling his responsibilities to his family or in his work: is no longer able to achieve anything. Delusional responses may include the conviction that the patient is totally worthless, or that he is an unbearable burden for his family, for his employers, or for the community in general.

31. **Hypochondriasis.** Excessive preoccupation with one's health or bodily functions. A rating of 3, delusional hypochondriasis, should be made if the patient describes an unshakeable conviction that he is suffering from an incurable disease, that his internal organs are "rotting away", etc. This conviction cannot be reversed by evidence to the contrary, and is obviously out of keeping with objective data on the patient's physical health.

Recommended probes:

- Do you tend to brood over your physical health?
- Do you think that you might have a serious physical disease?
- Are you troubled by the fear that your body and internal organs are not functioning properly?
- Do you spend more time now thinking about your physical health or how your body is working?

Examples of characteristic responses

Nondelusional hypochondriasis may include a continual excessive preoccupation with bodily or mental functions, self-observation, worries about the possibility of having one or more diseases, fears that one or more organs may be diseased. The patient, however, is responsive to persuasion to the contrary. Delusional responses may include the firm belief of the patient that he is incurably ill. Often the patients suggest a diagnosis of their disease—e.g., cancer, and describe a multitude of signs which to them are incontrovertible evidence of a fatal disease. Some patients describe bizarre beliefs—e.g., that their bowels or other internal organs are rotting away, or have been destroyed.

32. Ideas of impoverishment. The patient is excessively preoccupied with the idea that he might become poor, or his family destitute, or both. A rating of 3, delusional intensity of the symptom, should be made if the patient's belief that he is poor cannot be reversed by evidence to the contrary and is out of keeping with any realistic appraisal of his social and economic position.

Recommended probes:

● Are you afraid that you might run out of money, that you or your family may be financially ruined, or that you are being reduced to poverty?
● Are you afraid that you might lose all the money you have, that you might be left in the street with no means to live, or that your children will be left without money, clothes or shelter?

Examples of characteristic responses

Nondelusional responses may include feelings that the patient's property is valueless now or may lose its value in the future; fears that he or his family, or both, may starve, have no clothes or shelter, that he may be reduced to a beggar's existence in the future. Delusional responses may include the conviction (out of keeping with reality) that he is utterly impoverished, that his family is already bankrupt, that he has no choice but to live on charity or beg.

33. Ideas of reference and/or persecution

(a) **Ideas of reference.** The patient feels that specific events or actions of other people have a special meaning for him; e.g., someone's cough indicates that the patient is recognized as a criminal. A rating of 3, delusional ideas of reference, should be made if his belief that events have a special meaning for him cannot be reversed by evidence to the contrary, and is out of keeping with his social and cultural background.

Recommended probes:

● Do you feel on occasions that things other people say, or do, have a special meaning for you?
● Do you think that some of the things happening around you have been arranged especially for you?

Examples of characteristic responses

Nondelusional ideas of reference may include the feeling, lacking complete certainty, that others are talking about the patient, that particular happenings have a special bearing on his own person, that the radio or television is referring to him. Delusional responses may include the firm belief that people, newspapers, television, etc. are constantly exchanging messages about him.

(b) **Ideas of persecution.** Patient feels that people are against him, and may be trying to harm him deliberately. A rating of 3, delusions of persecution, should be made if the patient's false belief that he is being persecuted or harmed cannot be reversed by evidence to the contrary and is out of keeping with his social and cultural background.

Recommended probes:

- Do you think that you are being spied upon or persecuted by anyone—the police, your neighbours, or your fellow-workers, for example?
- Do you think that there may be a conspiracy of people trying to harm you in some way? How sure are you?

Examples of characteristic responses

Nondelusional responses may include description of feelings (without full conviction) that others in his family, at work, or in the community may be wanting to harm him. Delusional responses include the firm conviction of the patient that he is being hunted by individuals or organizations who wish to harm him; that he is the target of an elaborate plot; that people are concocting false evidence against him; that he is being spied upon, observed, etc. The patient tends to interpret minor everyday events as incontrovertible evidence for his belief.

34. **Other delusions.** Specify, describe briefly, and rate. This item includes religious delusions (e.g., selected by God for a special mission); delusions of catastrophe (e.g., belief in impending universal doom); sexual delusions (e.g., patient's sex being changed, or being pregnant by the devil); delusions of control by an external force; various delusional misinterpretations and misidentifications.

Recommended probes:

- Are there any other unusual experiences that have occurred, or any other ideas that occupy your mind, or cause concern? For example, is religion important to you? Do you think that you may have been singled out for a special mission on Earth? That your thoughts and movements may be controlled by an external force?

35. **Disorders of perception: illusions and hallucinations**

(a) **Illusion.** Mistaken perception, usually with affective undertones, of real objects, e.g., the patient experiences actual noises as human voices or cries; perceives patterns on the wall as faces. The experience may or may not be followed by a recognition of the perceptual mistake.

(b) **Hallucination.** False perception in *any sensory modality* that cannot be related to any identifiable stimulus. Regardless of their severity and frequency, hallucinations should be rated 3 when present; the rating should be supplemented by a brief note indicating the modality—e.g., "auditory", and content—e.g., "a voice talking to the patient accusing him of his misdeeds".

The interviewer should try to determine, first, whether the patient's perception followed an identifiable stimulus, and second, whether, if the stimulus is identifiable, the patient's perception was correct or incorrect.

Recommended probes:

● Do you ever hear noises or other sounds that other people cannot hear?
● Do you have visions or see things that other people cannot see?
● Do you smell some thing(s) that other people cannot?
● Do you feel things crawling over your skin? And when you look cannot find anything?

36. **Psychomotor retardation.** Slowness or lack of active movements, or decreased speed of response during interview. It should be noted that specific questions are not asked to elicit this symptom because the rating is based on observation of the patient's psychomotor activity.

Among possible observations

Patient has a low, monotonous voice, lacks facial expression, walks slowly, lacks spontaneous gestures, may be stuporous.

37. **Psychomotor restlessness and agitation.** Aimless motor overactivity. No questions are asked because the rating is based on observation of the patient's restlessness and agitation.

Among possible observations

Patient paces up and down, wrings hands, cannot sit still, cannot lie in bed, performs a series of activities without achieving a goal, e.g., scratches or rubs himself.

38. **Worse in the morning than at any other time during the day.** Patient feels that his depressive symptoms are more pronounced in the morning, and less pronounced during the day.

39. **Worse in the evening than at any other time during the day.** Patient feels that his depressive symptoms are more pronounced in the evening, and less pronounced during the morning.

Recommended probes for Items 38 and 39:

● When do you feel worse—in the morning or the evening?
● Is there any time during the day when you feel a little better?

Examples of characteristic responses

"Worse in the morning . . ." The patient wakes up feeling miserable, the coming day appears to him as an insurmountable obstacle. This feeling gradually lifts in the course of the day and he feels somewhat better toward the evening.

"Worse in the evening . . ." The patient feels particularly miserable in the evening, dreads bedtime. In the morning he feels less depressed.

It should be noted that if the symptom is present, little probing is necessary to elicit it. The experience is a quite distinct one, and patients are able to describe it clearly if it has occurred.

40. **Physical disease or infirmity.** Any physical disorder that has occurred at the same time as or after the onset of the episode being assessed. The investigator should inquire about diagnosis, treatment, and consultations given when judging whether an illness or disability is present. It should be noted that somatic signs and symptoms not associated with an identifiable physical illness or disability are rated in Item 24.

Recommended probes:

These should be about widespread conditions—e.g., heart disease, arthritis, diabetes in some settings; infectious diseases and their consequences in others.

Part 2B. Psychiatric history

41. **History of psychiatric disorder (affective) in blood relatives.** Affective disorders include: depressive and manic episodes, and personality disorder with pronounced mood abnormalities (e.g., cyclothymic mood swings, persistent depressive or hypomanic mood). Also rate present if either suicide attempts or suicides have occurred. History of affective disorders should be rated as present in patient's parents, grandparents, siblings, children, or parents' siblings, if there is evidence that the disorder required psychiatric treatment or disrupted the patient's behaviour and social functioning. It is necessary to specify which relative(s) was(were) affected.

Recommended probes:

● Have any of your relatives ever suffered from depression—e.g., was very sad, unhappy, or cried often for periods of at least 2 weeks at a time?
● Have any of your relatives ever attempted suicide or committed suicide?
● Have any of your relatives been high—i.e., much more active than usual for at least 2 weeks?
● Do you have any relatives who have or have had problems like yours?
● Were they ever treated?
● How did this problem affect his/her life?

42. **History of psychiatric disorder (other) in blood relatives.** Evidence of other psychiatric disorders should be recorded here: for example, schizophrenia, severe personality disorder other than the types specified in Item 41, neuroses, epilepsy, alcohol or drug dependence, organic psychoses, and mental retardation. The item should be rated as present for any of the patient's parents, grandparents, siblings, children, and parents' siblings if there is adequate evidence—e.g., if the disorder required psychiatric treatment or if, according to the patient or an informant, it disrupted the patient's behaviour or social functioning. The relative(s) affected should be specified in the schedule.

Recommended probes:

● Have any of your relatives had emotional problems or a nervous breakdown?
● Have any of your relatives been treated by a psychiatrist or admitted to hospital for a drinking problem, problems with drugs, epilepsy, schizophrenia, or any other reason?

43. Early separation. This history item should be rated as present if the patient or an informant reports that family disruption was caused by the absence of one or both parents or parent-substitutes for at least one continuous year before the patient was 6 years old.

Recommended probes:

● During your early childhood, were you ever separated from either your mother or your father, or both, for any length of time, i.e., at least one year? If so, how old were you when the separation occurred?
● Did it cause any problems in your family life?

44. Stressful events in early childhood. Should be rated as present if the patient, before 6 years of age, had been exposed to any one of four situations:

(*a*) One or both parents, or another person in continual contact with the patient, had a severe personality disorder or a psychotic condition, or was dependent on alcohol or other drugs;

(*b*) Was definitely mistreated, e.g., often brutally punished;

(*c*) Was consistently deprived of adequate food, shelter, or clothing to an extent not commensurate with his household's income;

(*d*) Continual severe friction prevailed between parents or parent-substitutes with whom the patient lived.

The nature of the stressful event(s) should be specified in a brief narrative.

Recommended probes:

The interviewer should begin with a general question, e.g., Were there any events in your early childhood that you think were particularly stressful for you? Following this, the investigator should inquire specifically whether the patient was exposed to any of the situations described above.

45. Psychopathological symptoms in childhood. Rate as present if the patient reports that he suffered from at least one of the following conditions before 14 years of age:

(*a*) Speech disturbances, e.g., stuttering or stammering (after the age of 3);

(*b*) Tics, i.e., involuntary, localized sudden muscle contractions not caused by known neurological lesions;

(*c*) Sleep disorders, e.g., sleep walking, frequent night terrors;

(*d*) Enuresis, i.e., habitual bedwetting, at least once a month, after the patient's sixth birthday;

(*e*) Frequent or persistent absence from school for reasons other than physical disease or environmental restrictions;

(*f*) Frequent running away from home for a day or more, without permission;

(*g*) Psychiatric disorder requiring treatment or frequent psychiatric consultation.

Recommended probes:

The interviewer should ask a general question first e.g., Do you remember, or were you ever told, that as a child you had problems? Following this, he should inquire about the occurrence of the symptoms listed above.

46. **Psychopathological symptoms in adolescence.** Psychiatric symptoms, syndromes, or abnormal social behaviour, e.g., the patient's behaviour was clearly different from that of his peers between the ages of 14 and 20. It should be remembered that definite depressive or manic episodes should not be rated here but in Items 51 and 53.

Examples of conditions that should be explored here:

(*a*) Anorexia nervosa;

(*b*) Reactive confusion;

(*c*) Nonaffective psychoses;

(*d*) Firesetting behaviour;

(*e*) Serious phobic states;

(*f*) Over-reaction to everyday events, e.g., running away from home, even briefly, because of a poor school report;

(*g*) Severe neurotic symptoms, e.g., hysterical blindness, severe obsessional symptoms.

Recommended probes:

A general question should be asked first, e.g., Did you have any emotional problems in adolescence? The investigator should then inquire about the occurrence of specific symptoms, syndromes, or abnormal behaviour.

47. **Psychopathological symptoms and syndromes in adult life other than past or present affective disturbances.** Any psychiatric symptoms and syndromes experienced by the patient in adult life (from age 20 on) but before the present episode, for example:

(*a*) Nonaffective endogenous and exogenous psychoses;

(*b*) Neuroses (other than depressive);

(*c*) Alcohol or drug dependence or severe abuse causing problems to patient and/or his family;

(*d*) Psychosomatic symptoms unrelated to depression;

(*e*) Epilepsy.

Definite manic and depressive episodes should be rated in Items 51 and 53 and mood swings associated with personality disorders (e.g., cyclothymic personality) should be rated in Item 48.

Recommended probes:

A general question should be asked first, e.g., Have you experienced any mental or emotional problems in your adult life apart from depression or mania? Then, if the answer is "yes", the investigator should inquire about the occurrence of specific symptoms or syndromes.

48. Pronounced traits of premorbid personality. Patient experiences psychological or social adjustment problems caused by disorders of personality structure. These problems should be longstanding and be present outside periods of psychiatric illness, including the present episode. They may include:

(*a*) Anancastic personality disorder;
(*b*) Hysterical personality disorder;
(*c*) Explosive personality disorder;
(*d*) Antisocial behaviour associated with abnormal personality traits;
(*e*) Schizoid personality disorder;
(*f*) Cyclothymic personality.

Recommended probes:

Begin with a general question, e.g., Do you feel that apart from your present illness your own personality and way of interacting with people have caused you problems? If relevant, the interviewer should inquire about the presence of the disorders listed above.

49. Continual psychic stress. Any situation or condition existing continuously or intermittently for months or years before the current episode that the patient or an informant considers stressful. The stressful situation(s) associated with the current episode may include:

(*a*) Situational stress, e.g., employment difficulties;
(*b*) Social stress, e.g., difficulties with neighbours, housing difficulties, economic difficulties;
(*c*) Family stress, e.g., continuous marital discord, difficulties with in-laws;
(*d*) Psychosexual stress, e.g., continuous and disturbing lack of sexual satisfaction with partner;
(*e*) Physical stress, e.g., chronic physical handicap.

Recommended probes:

Begin with a general question, e.g., Have you been under stress or strain for a long time? If the answer is positive, inquire about specific stresses using the list above as a guide.

50. **Precipitating stress.** An event or experience in the patient's life which:

(a) Has occurred within 6 months of the current episode;
(b) Is recognized by the patient or informant as stressful; and
(c) Is related by content to the development of symptoms of the current episode.

Since events affect people differently, it is necessary to inquire about the individual's particular response to an event, which may have made that experience stressful—e.g., a promotion at work may be accepted as giving opportunity for further advancement, or may be feared because of the increased responsibility it brings. The nature of the precipitating stress should be specified.

Recommended probes:

Ask a general question first, e.g., Do you think that a specific stressful event or experience played a part at the start of this episode? Then inquire further according to the guidelines above.

51. **Number of previous depressive episodes.** Rate the number of previous depressive episodes. For a pattern of symptoms to be considered an episode, three criteria must be met:

(a) At least two of the symptoms given as inclusion criteria in the Screening Form should have been present;
(b) The symptoms should be of at least 2 weeks' duration;
(c) A period of at least 30 days without any depressive symptoms (a free interval) should precede and follow the period during which depressive symptoms were present.

Untreated depressive episodes should also be counted if the above criteria are met. However, normal grief reactions should be excluded. Rate 00 if no previous episodes, 88 if information on past episodes is impossible to obtain, and 99 if there is clear evidence of past depressive episodes, but no estimate of their number is possible. "Doubtful" episodes should not be rated here, but in Item 47.

Recommended probes:

● Have you had mood swings in the past?
● How bad were they?
● How many times have you felt depressed in your life?
● How many depressions have you had before this one?

52. **Number of years since first depressive episode.** Rate the number of years since the beginning of the patient's first depressive episode.

(*Note.* Rate 88 if Item 51 was rated 00—no episodes, and 99 if the number of years is unknown.)

Recommended probe:

● How long has it been since your first depression?

53. **Number of previous manic episodes.** Rate number of previous manic episodes. For a pattern of symptoms to be considered an episode, three criteria must be met:

(*a*) Symptoms and signs such as persistently elevated mood, hyperactivity, grandiose behaviour, interference with others, and lack of sleep should be present;

(*b*) The episode should be of at least 2 weeks' duration;

(*c*) A period of at least 30 days without any symptoms of mania should precede and follow the period during which manic symptoms were present.

If the patient has had an acute manic episode followed by an acute depressive episode, without a 30-day interval, the disorder should be regarded as one discrete episode rather than two. Untreated manic episodes should also be counted, if criteria are met. Rate 00 if no previous episodes, and 88 if no information is available on the number of manic episodes but there is evidence that they have occurred. "Doubtful" episodes should be rated in Item 47.

Recommended probes:

The interviewer might ask a general question first, e.g., Have there been periods in your life when you felt much more cheerful and were much more active and enterprising than usual? Then, inquire concerning the criteria above.

54. **Number of years since first manic episode.** Rate the number of years since the beginning of the patient's first manic episode.

(*Note.* Rate 88 if Item 53 was rated 00—no episodes, 99 if the number of years is unknown.)

Recommended probe:

● How long has it been since your first manic attack?

55. **Number of intervals free of symptoms.** An interval should be rated as present if there has been at least 2 weeks' duration between depressive episodes, or between consecutive episodes of mania and depression, when the patient is completely free of depressive or manic symptoms. During an interval, the patient may either be entirely symptom-free or exhibit mild or nonspecific symptoms that are clearly not part of either a depressive or a manic episode. Such symptoms may include, for example, accentuated personality traits such as obsessional thoughts. If the patient has no depressive or manic symptoms even though he is receiving psychiatric treatment or taking psychotropic medication, or both, he is considered to be in an interval. Rate 88 if no previous episodes, 99 if the number of intervals is unknown.

Recommended probes:

The interviewer should inquire specifically what symptoms, if any, were present after each depressive or manic episode and reconstruct the course of illness before rating.

56. **Type of onset of current episode.** Types of onset may be:

(a) Clearly sudden (less than 2 weeks from first symptom to full development of present condition);
(b) Slow or insidious;
(c) Not clear or unknown.

This item is often difficult to rate. If any uncertainty persists after sufficient explanation, the suggested rating is 9. Ratings 1 and 2 should be used only when a clear description of sudden or slow onset are given.

Recommended probes:

● How did this illness start?
● Did it come on suddenly, within a few days, or did it start slowly, gradually?

57. **Duration of present condition.** Rate with reference to the likely time of onset of symptoms that are definitely part of the present episode. The onset of symptoms may have preceded the start of psychiatric treatment; rate according to the onset of symptoms. Do not rate the presence of personality traits here.

Recommended probe:

● When did you first notice you were not feeling well?

Example: A 50-year-old woman presented for treatment 2 weeks ago. Her history reveals that although she was free of abnormal personality traits, she experienced anxiety, insomnia, and psychosomatic symptoms 8 years ago. Three months ago, she suddenly (within 4 or 5 days) became depressed and suicidal. Rate 2.

PART 3. TREATMENT IN PRESENT EPISODE

Items 3.1–3.7 inclusive are self-explanatory. It is important to specify drug used and dosage. Rate present if given in present episode, even if discontinued and not taken at point of interview.

3.8 **Psychotherapy.** Do not include here simple contact with patients, e.g., short discussions during ward rounds or consultations, that are not part of a systematic plan of psychotherapy.

3.9 **Other.** For example, behaviour therapy, traditional healing.

PART 4. DIAGNOSIS AND CLASSIFICATION

4.1 **Psychiatrist's clinical assessment of the overall severity of the condition.** This item refers to the present episode of depressive symptomatology. The severity of a depressive state can be assessed on more than one dimension, or aspect, of the condition and there is no general agreement about the criteria to be used. In making a clinical judgement about the rating of severity, it is recommended that the following guidelines be used:

Mild. A depressive syndrome is definitely present but features like marked retardation, agitation, delusions, or suicidal ideation are absent. The patient is able to cope with the demands of daily life, though with difficulty.

Moderate. Retardation, or agitation, anergia, ideas of inadequacy and experience of inefficiency, as well as other ideas of depressive content are present, but not delusions. Fleeting thoughts about life not being worth living may be present, but no specific thoughts or plans of committing suicide. This state interferes seriously with the patient's daily routine, without incapacitating him entirely.

Severe. Very marked retardation or agitation; presence of depressive delusions; suicidal thoughts, plans, and/or actions. The social functioning of the patient is seriously disturbed or practically arrested.

Very severe. As above, but with elements of a threat to the patient's survival: stupor and/or persistent refusal of food; uncontrollable agitation and/or suicidal impulsive actions (*raptus melancholicus*). A rating of "very severe" depression can also be made in the absence of clear life-threatening signs if the rater has other reasons to believe that the depressive illness is of a nature that endangers the patient's life or the lives of others.

If a rating of "severe" or "very severe" is made, it is recommended that the reasons for making it be specified in a brief narrative note in the schedule.

4.2 **State diagnosis according to your own practice.** A diagnosis (and, if relevant, a differential and/or supplementary diagnosis) should be entered in a narrative, in the way that is customary to the rater with regard to preferred diagnostic and classification system, terminology, etc.

4.3 **How would you classify your diagnosis according to the Ninth Revision of the International Classification of Diseases?** It is recommended that the glossary incorporated in Chapter 5 (Mental Disorders) of the Ninth Revision of the ICD[1] should always be used. The five spaces provided for four-digit codes should be used as follows:

1. (43–46) Main diagnosis. This code is mandatory.
2. (47–50) Alternatative diagnosis (optional). If no alternative diagnosis is made, enter 0000.

---

[1] WORLD HEALTH ORGANIZATION. *Manual of the International Statistical Classification of Diseases, Injuries, and Causes of Death,* 1975 (Ninth) Revision, Geneva, Volumes 1 and 2, 1977 and 1978. See also: *Mental disorders: Glossary and guide to their classification in accordance with the Ninth Revision of the International Classification of Diseases.* Geneva, World Health Organization, 1978.

3. (51–54) Supplementary psychiatric diagnosis (optional). This space should be used for coding any psychiatric condition (i.e., one listed in Chapter 5 of ICD-9) that accompanies or underlies the condition recorded as main diagnosis—for example, 303 (alcohol dependence syndrome)—but is not an alternative to it. If no supplementary psychiatric diagnosis is made, enter 0000.

4. (55–58) Other supplementary diagnosis—not psychiatric (optional). This space should be used to code any other disorder, outside Chapter 5 of ICD-9, that is present and is considered sufficiently important to warrant recording. If a physical illness or condition is thought to have a causal relationship with the psychiatric condition(s) recorded above, it should be coded here. If this space is not used, enter 0000.

5. (59–62) Other supplementary diagnosis—not psychiatric (optional). This space allows the coding of a second nonpsychiatric condition, if relevant. If this space is not used, code 0000.

WHO publications may be obtained, direct or through booksellers, from:

ALGERIA	Société Nationale d'Edition et de Diffusion, 3 bd Zirout Youcef, ALGIERS
ARGENTINA	Carlos Hirsch SRL, Florida 165, Galerías Güemes, Escritorio 453/465, BUENOS AIRES
AUSTRALIA	Hunter Publications, 58A Gipps Street, COLLINGWOOD, VIC 3066 — Australian Government Publishing Service *(Mail order sales)*, P.O. Box 84, CANBERRA A.C.T. 2600; *or over the counter from:* Australian Government Publishing Service Bookshops *at:* 70 Alinga Street, CANBERRA CITY A.C.T. 2600; 294 Adelaide Street, BRISBANE, Queensland 4000; 347 Swanston Street, MELBOURNE, VIC 3000; 309 Pitt Street, SYDNEY, N.S.W. 2000; Mt Newman House, 200 St. George's Terrace, PERTH, WA 6000; Industry House, 12 Pirie Street, ADELAIDE, SA 5000; 156–162 Macquarie Street, HOBART, TAS 7000 — R. Hill & Son Ltd., 608 St. Kilda Road, MELBOURNE, VIC 3004; Lawson House, 10–12 Clark Street, CROW'S NEST, NSW 2065
AUSTRIA	Gerold & Co., Graben 31, 1011 VIENNA I
BANGLADESH	The WHO Programme Coordinator, G.P.O. Box 250, DACCA 5 — The Association of Voluntary Agencies, P.O. Box 5045, DACCA 5
BELGIUM	Office international de Librairie, 30 avenue Marnix, 1050 BRUSSELS — *Subscriptions to World Health only:* Jean de Lannoy, 202 avenue du Roi, 1060 BRUSSELS
BRAZIL	Biblioteca Regional de Medicina OMS/OPS, Unidade de Venda de Publicações, Caixa Postal 20.381, Vila Clementino, 04023 SÃO PAULO, S.P.
BURMA	*see* India, WHO Regional Office
CANADA	Canadian Public Health Association, 1335 Carling Avenue, Suite 210, OTTAWA, Ont. K1Z 8N8. *Subscriptions: Subscription orders, accompanied by cheque made out to the* Royal Bank of Canada, Ottawa, Account World Health Organization, *may also be sent to the* World Health Organization, P.O. Box 1800, Postal Station B, OTTAWA, Ont. K1P 5R5
CHINA	China National Publications Import & Export Corporation, P.O. Box 88, BEIJING (PEKING)
COLOMBIA	Distrilibros Ltd., Pio Alfonso Garcia, Carrera 4a, Nos 36–119, CARTAGENA
CYPRUS	"MAM", P.O. Box 1722, NICOSIA
CZECHO- SLOVAKIA	Artia, Ve Smeckach 30, 111 27 PRAGUE I
DENMARK	Munksgaard Export and Subscription Service, Nørre Søgade 35, 1370 COPENHAGEN K (Tel: +45 1 12 85 70)
ECUADOR	Libreria Cientifica S.A., P.O. Box 362, Luque 223, GUAYAQUIL
EGYPT	Osiris Office for Books and Reviews, 50 Kasr El Nil Street, CAIRO
EL SALVADOR	Libreria Estudiantil, Edificio Comercial B No 3, Avenida Libertad, SAN SALVADOR
FIJI	The WHO Programme Coordinator, P.O. Box 113, SUVA
FINLAND	Akateeminen Kirjakauppa, Keskuskatu 2, 00101 HELSINKI 10
FRANCE	Librairie Arnette, 2 rue Casimir-Delavigne, 75006 PARIS
GERMAN DEMOCRATIC REPUBLIC	Buchhaus Leipzig, Postfach 140, 701 LEIPZIG
GERMANY, FEDERAL REPUBLIC OF	Govi-Verlag GmbH, Ginnheimerstrasse 20, Postfach 5360, 6236 ESCHBORN — W. E. Saarbach, Postfach 101 610, Follerstrasse 2, 5000 COLOGNE I — Alex. Horn, Spiegelgasse 9, Postfach 3340, 6200 WIESBADEN
GHANA	Fides Enterprises, P.O. Box 1628, ACCRA
GREECE	G.C. Eleftheroudakis S.A., Librairie internationale, rue Nikis 4, ATHENS (T. 126)
HAITI	Max Bouchereau, Librairie "A la Caravelle", Boîte postale 111-B, PORT-AU-PRINCE
HONG KONG	Hong Kong Government Information Services, Beaconsfield House, 6th Floor, Queen's Road, Central, VICTORIA
HUNGARY	Kultura, P.O.B. 149, BUDAPEST 62 — Akadémiai Könyvesbolt, Váci utca 22, BUDAPEST V
ICELAND	Snaebjørn Jonsson & Co., P.O. Box 1131, Hafnarstraeti 9, REYKJAVIK
INDIA	WHO Regional Office for South-East Asia, World Health House, Indraprastha Estate, Mahatma Gandhi Road, NEW DELHI 110002 — Oxford Book & Stationery Co., Scindia House, NEW DELHI 110001; 17 Park Street, CALCUTTA 700016 (*Sub-agent*)
INDONESIA	P. T. Kalman Media Pusaka, Pusat Perdagangan Senen, Block 1, 4th Floor, P.O. Box 3433/Jkt, JAKARTA
IRAQ	Ministry of Information, National House for Publishing, Distributing and Advertising, BAGHDAD
IRELAND	TDC Publishers, 12 North Frederick Street, DUBLIN 1
ISRAEL	Heiliger & Co., 3 Nathan Strauss Street, JERUSALEM
ITALY	Edizioni Minerva Medica, Corso Bramante 83–85, 10126 TURIN; Via Lamarmora 3, 20100 MILAN
JAPAN	Maruzen Co. Ltd., P.O. Box 5050, TOKYO International, 100–31
KOREA REPUBLIC OF	The WHO Programme Coordinator, Central P.O. Box 540, SEOUL
KUWAIT	The Kuwait Bookshops Co. Ltd., Thunayan Al-Ghanem Bldg, P.O. Box 2942, KUWAIT
LAO PEOPLE'S DEMOCRATIC REPUBLIC	The WHO Programme Coordinator, P.O. Box 343, VIENTIANE
LEBANON	The Levant Distributors Co. S.A.R.L., Box 1181, Makdassi Street, Hanna Bldg, BEIRUT
LUXEMBOURG	Librairie du Centre, 49 bd Royal, LUXEMBOURG